Praise for *The Mindfulness Code*

"*The Mindfulness Code* is like having your own personal mindfulness coach. Altman's joy, passion, and knowledge are evident in each of the book's clearly written experiential teachings. This book cannot help but bring more joy, happiness, and contentment to the lives of everyone who reads it. It is a much-needed elixir for these turbulent times."

— Randall Fitzgerald, author of *The Hundred-Year Lie* and former roving editor for *Reader's Digest*

"Donald Altman's latest book is a feast of kindness, wisdom, humor, and insight. Each chapter offers practical and inspiring ways to cultivate inner peace amid everyday life. It's a beautifully written book that readers will want to savor as well as share with others. Once you start cracking *The Mindfulness Code*, you won't want to stop."

— Ronna Kabatznick, PhD, assistant clinical professor at Langley Porter Psychiatric Institute, University of California, San Francisco

"For those looking for more meaning from work or at work, *The Mindfulness Code* opens the door to discovering how you can derive more satisfaction from what you do. Happiness, as Altman explains, can come from what you do for yourself as well as for others. The four keys to *The Mindfulness Code* are enlightening but also practical, especially when coupled with the more than forty strategies presented in this easy-to-read text. *The Mindfulness Code* is a book that you will find yourself reaching for again and again as you explore meaning in your own life's work."

— John Baldoni, author of *Lead Your Boss* and *Lead By Example*

"There are books about mindfulness as a technique for solving this or that problem. And then there are books that unpack the bigger-picture treasures of *mindfulness as a worldview. The Mindfulness*

Code is an open-source secret of mindful living, a compassionate invitation to infuse mindfulness into every aspect of one's life. In offering a set of four keys for overcoming suffering, Altman remains an ever-skillful locksmith, narrating an innovative existential map with the help of teachings, inspirations, clinical vignettes, personal revelations, and ready-to-use techniques."

— Pavel Somov, PhD, author of
Present Perfect: Letting Go of Perfectionism and the Need to Control

"*The Mindfulness Code* richly integrates ancient body-mind-spirit knowledge with cutting-edge brain science. The book is filled with evidence-based research practices designed to relieve suffering caused by anxiety, depression, and life difficulties. Individuals and therapists alike will benefit from these simple, realistic, and achievable tools that are necessary for rebuilding one's life with hope, resilience, and gratitude."

— Greg Crosby, MA, LPC, CGP, trainer, psychotherapist,
and faculty member at Portland State University
and Marylhurst University

"*The Mindfulness Code* is a wonderful mix of warmth, humor, and gentle wisdom. Donald Altman weaves an engrossing blend of insights and personal stories from his many years as a skilled therapist along with illustrative research findings and many helpful mindfulness exercises. This book will hand you the keys for unlocking a life of greater ease and happiness."

— Zen Roshi Jan Chozen Bays, MD,
author of *Mindful Eating* and *A Year of Mindful Living*

THE MINDFULNESS CODE

Also by Donald Altman

Art of the Inner Meal

Living Kindness

Meal by Meal

THE MINDFULNESS CODE

Keys for Overcoming Stress,
Anxiety, Fear, and Unhappiness

DONALD ALTMAN

New World Library
Novato, California

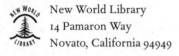

New World Library
14 Pamaron Way
Novato, California 94949

For permission acknowledgments, see pages 163 and 207.
Text design by Tona Pearce Myers

Library of Congress Cataloging-in-Publication Data
Altman, Don, date.
The mindfulness code : keys for overcoming stress, anxiety, fear, and unhappiness / Donald Altman.
   p.   cm.
Includes bibliographical references and index.
ISBN 978-1-57731-893-4 (pbk. : alk. paper)
1. Stress (Psychology) 2. Stress management. 3. Mind and body. I. Title.
BF575.S75A48 2010
158—dc22   2010005432

First printing, June 2010
ISBN 978-1-57731-893-4
Printed in Canada on 100% postconsumer-waste recycled paper

 New World Library is a proud member of the Green Press Initiative.

10 9 8 7 6 5 4 3 2 1

This book is dedicated to peace
and all who seek peace,
within and without.

May each grain of mindfulness
be a blessing of awakening
on behalf of all who suffer.

May each grain of mindfulness
be an instrument of peace and love
for the benefit and well-being of all.

Contents

Introduction

*H*AVE YOU EVER DREAMED OF LIVING IN AN AGE or a place that offers the promise of a simpler life? A place where friendship and kindness flourish? Where peace and silence are close at hand? Where innumerable joys are waiting to be found? Believe it or not, you needn't search for the legendary kingdom of Shambhala to find such peace and tranquility. It is very real, and it exists in the midst of our complex twenty-first-century life, in a nearby land known as the here and now. But the land of here and now — with its treasures of deep peace, joy, and awareness — is often hidden from view and hard to find. Mindfulness is the master key that opens the door to these inner riches, and you need only unlock your natural birthright of mindful awareness to gain entry.

There has probably never been another period in the history of humankind as frenetic, hectic, fast, and chaotic as our own. As much as we collectively embrace and marvel at the speed, connections, and benefits of technology, we need also to acknowledge the effects of its complexity and costs — most significantly, perpetually high levels of stress. Chronic stress has been implicated in a majority of illnesses. In the United States, at least 50 percent of all medications are for conditions related to chronic stress. Worldwide levels of depression, anxiety, and addiction have reached unprecedented heights; one in four persons on the planet are estimated to be clinically depressed. These are just a few of the signposts (more like Vegas-style flashing neon billboards) telling us that we as a species are out of balance.

I wrote *The Mindfulness Code* as an antidote for those who sense that their lives are either empty or out of balance and want something more. If you can't seem to slow down, if your life is congested and cluttered, if your thoughts exhaust and sabotage you, or if you are without enough time and energy to do what you really want, then *The Mindfulness Code* can give you practical strategies to turn things around.

Mindfulness as explored in these pages is more than simply being in the present moment. It is the means of peering into the true nature of our own greed and attachment, delusion and ignorance, and avoidance and fear, which all lead to suffering. As humans, each of us struggles to get beyond our binding negative emotions and cravings. This doesn't mean that we are flawed or bad. Mindfulness is not a moralistic approach designed to help us find our "good" or "better" self. What mindfulness provides is the opportunity to experience a less encumbered and less entangled state of being and awareness.

Ironically, you can't use the mind you presently have — the one that is already battle weary, harried, fearful, preoccupied, and crammed with thoughts of planning, fretting, and regretting — to help you figure a way out of this mess. Mindfulness, though, lets you explore your life in an entirely new way. Instead of being possessed by the thoughts, feelings, objects, and events in your life, you learn to *observe and to examine* these in a nonthreatening way — with a sense of spaciousness that engenders stillness, openness, acceptance, harmony, peace, and joy. To do this is to activate the mindful brain you already possess but have forgotten how or never learned to use.

Fortunately, the brain is extremely adaptable and capable of rewiring itself through mindfulness practices. Those who meditate have suspected this for years. Today, thanks to recent brain imaging studies of monks and others who practice mindfulness, scientific evidence shows that *thoughts alone can shape the brain at the physical level.* Throughout *The Mindfulness Code,* I share important brain research on how mindfulness actually helps and encourages our best efforts — how it loosens and transforms old habits, negative thoughts, and harmful beliefs from the inside out.

The Mindfulness Code offers a vastly different approach for dealing with life's problems than that endorsed by many in the conventional medical community — those who spend millions of dollars on medications that reduce negative feelings in the body and mind by altering neurotransmitter levels in the brain, which is how drugs such as Prozac and Xanax work. Of course, there are times when conventional medication can help over the short term, depending on the severity of the condition. I learned this personally when struggling with clinical depression in my early twenties. Although I was prescribed Valium, I rarely took it — only when I needed to be reminded what it felt like not to be severely depressed and hopeless. Used sparingly, it was useful. I have rarely been depressed since and never clinically (contrary to research that suggests that clinical depression is recurring). I believe my depression didn't return because I began to engage in various practices for *intentionally centering attention now* — practices that helped me to observe my mind and train it not to attach too strongly to the thoughts and feelings that pop up. *Intentionally Centering Attention Now*, or *I-CAN*, is a broad term I created to describe how mindfulness and meditation work to regulate our emotions, which in turn nurtures joy, aliveness, and flexibility in our experience. As you explore the mindfulness teachings and strategies in this book, you will experience four catalyzing qualities of living awareness.

Intention, the first quality, is the goal-setting aspect of mind that is necessary for us to be effective. It means we can be purposeful in using awareness. Everything we have achieved or brought into our life came about through an intention we set — from finding a job or a relationship to getting an education or a new car. Intention is the engine of effort; it provides the initial spark of energy, enthusiasm, vision, and purpose. By engaging our attention to be more awake and aware, we step off the ingrained path of old habits and ruts. Intention as used in *The Mindfulness Code* is a powerful change agent.

Centering, the second quality, is about maintaining homeostasis between the body and the brain — much as a thermostat works to help an air conditioner or a furnace maintain a constant, comfortable temperature. Through centering, we learn how to better identify and respond to the stresses of the inner and outer worlds we inhabit — the inner world of thoughts, judgments, perceptions, appetites, desires, and emotions, and the outer world of diverse environments, activities, stimuli, and stressors. Centering is about fostering a compassionate and spacious attitude toward all our experiences and emotions. An open and compassionate attitude can help us locate peace, balance, flow, harmony, equanimity, and hope. By centering, we avoid becoming ensnared by the extremes of compulsive desire, attachment, and grasping, on the one hand, and avoidance, aversion, and fear, on the other. Centering means not that we can always change unwanted hardships, but that we more readily accept and engage with the difficulties of life.

The third quality, *attention*, involves several ways of learning how to sharpen some of the mind's beneficial innate faculties. This begins with cultivating a neutral and nonjudgmental awareness, which allows us to witness and observe events without attaching to them. Harnessing attention is also necessary to concentrate and sustain focus, to establish purposeful intention, and to cultivate a deep curiosity of all things through observation. At the practical level, attention is a necessary life skill that enables us to complete tasks and to locate resources. Attention is also vital for contemplation, insight, and wisdom to occur. In a world where diverse media sources seek to grab our attention, mastery of attention is a treasure worth cultivating and protecting.

The final catalyzing quality, *now*, is vital for genuinely experiencing and participating in the moment. The now captures our sense of being alive and stimulates our capacities for wonder and joy. It makes possible the vast openness of heart and mind that is required for flexibility of thought and action in each new moment. By being fluid and flexible, we can escape the filter of old habits or mental programs that impose themselves on the present moment. The value of adaptability also means that *there is no one way to experience Intentionally Centering Attention Now*. The combination of these four complementary qualities — intention, centering, attention, and presence in the now — makes the mindfulness strategies in these pages refreshing, empowering, and healthy approaches to balancing emotions and thoughts — and neurotransmitters.

It's All About the Connections

While the human brain and body have changed little in the past one hundred thousand years, the technological advances of just the past one hundred years have literally outpaced our ability to adapt to them. In *The Mindfulness Code*, you will learn how the brain can be used to maintain a healthy life-balance, despite being part of what I fondly refer to as "Generation Text." You may also begin to ponder the current 24/7 work ethic and lifestyle, the disappearance of darkness and silence in many areas of our planet, and the astonishing increase in the industrialization, efficiency, and speed of living, which combine to greatly diminish — perhaps threaten — the most profound connections we have available to us as a human community.

Two basic types of connection echo throughout *The Mindfulness Code*. One involves our connections with nature and the nonhuman world — ancient and timeless sources from which our ancestors found wisdom, solace, meaning, appreciation, awe, gratitude, humility, and the divine, as well as a healing repository for mind-body-spirit. In various ways, *The Mindfulness Code* explores how to find and strengthen nature-oriented connections in order to achieve a state of balance and inner calm.

The second type of connection involves our relationships with others — connections that do no less than shape the myriad of delicate neural networks in our own brains. These internal brain connections literally determine how we experience the world. The newest studies in brain science teach us that who we are, in great part, depends on the quality of our face-to-face relationships. When relationships are nurturing, enriching, positive, safe, and secure, the result is a brain that is not only more trusting but also more capable of communicating with others to get its needs met. Such a brain will also be competent at empathy, compassion, and knowing what others are feeling. These abilities are actually brain-wired capabilities that take time to develop — especially in young brains. Cutting-edge research noted throughout *The Mindfulness Code* suggests that if the brain does not build these interpersonal neural networks, then the ability to empathize (for example, to comprehend facial expressions) may very well be blunted. Attention may be fragmented, and emotions may be either numbed or extremely difficult to control.

Also, the psychological effects of an overstimulating environment are finally being investigated in a variety of ways; for example, a recent study by the American Psychological Association, which created a Task Force on the Sexualization of Girls in Media, examined the effects of sexual images in all forms of media — from music videos to print and television — on girls and young women.[1] Not surprisingly, the report found that this vulnerable population (actually, all our brains are vulnerable) was likely to suffer from low self-esteem, depressed mood or clinical depression, and eating disorders.

The mindfulness strategies in this book are designed to restore our vital connections. Instead of letting the overwhelming number of visual, auditory, and other sensory messages reaching us on a daily basis condition us to perceive and desire things in ways that satisfy big business, we can choose to foster self-awareness, discernment, kindness, and happiness. To be mindful is to recognize that our brains are affected and shaped at the physical level by what we choose to place our awareness and attention on.

My psychotherapy clients are greatly relieved when I tell them there is a natural way to return inner balance and harmony to the body and mind. Once we learn to stop fighting with the mind and allow it to be still, we discover that the mind has a calm, refined, and pure capacity to lead us toward a deep and abiding sense of happiness and serenity. *The Mindfulness Code* offers a hopeful and effective way of coping with the stress of twenty-first-century life. As the Buddha states in the Dhammapada, which translates as "the path of truth":

> *Mind is forerunner of all actions.*
> *All deeds are led by mind, created by mind.*
> *If one speaks or acts with a corrupt mind,*
> *suffering follows,*
> *As the wheel follows the hoof of an ox pulling a cart.*

> *Mind is forerunner of all actions.*
> *All deeds are led by mind, created by mind.*
> *If one speaks or acts with a serene mind,*
> *happiness follows,*
> *As surely as one's shadow.*[2]

Four Keys to Unlock Mindfulness

Mindfulness often seems indecipherable to those who are trying to grasp it for the first time. I often liken mindfulness to the air: it is all around us yet invisible at the same time. My intention with *The Mindfulness Code* is to make mindfulness, or ways of Intentionally Centering Attention Now, tangible. To this end, I present four keys for directly realizing moment-by-moment awareness: the mind key, the body key, the spirit key, and the relationship key. Each touches the heart of mindfulness and will illuminate the areas of your life in which you can experience deeper levels of awareness.

This book is divided into four parts, one corresponding to each key. You may work with one key until it is completed or move between keys. Each key contains eleven practical strategies for experiencing a fundamentally different way of being and living. Each is a self-contained mindfulness training and practice. Use a strategy as often as necessary. There are forty-four strategies in all; I recommend that you take your time getting to know each one. These trainings are not intended to carve up your day or to add more to an already busy schedule. Rather, the trainings are intended to help you become more awake to the life you are already living. You will quickly learn to locate calm, peace, and joy within each moment — even in the midst of chaos, congestion, and clutter.

Part 1, "The Mind Key," introduces strategies to change your brain from the inside out. By directly observing and experiencing mental phenomena — the transient nature of thoughts, beliefs, emotions, perceptions, and identity that shape our mental and psychological reality — you will rewire your brain and gain a new perspective on difficult feelings such as sadness, anger, jealousy, and despair. The strategies presented here include the happiness-producing practice of loving-kindness, deep acceptance of the moment, and ancient methods for priming the reactive and anxious brain for greater peace, security, and trust.

Part 2, "The Body Key," focuses on using the body to return home to the moment. No matter how stuck in the past or the future your mind and thoughts may be, each time you consciously inhabit the body, you touch the here and now in a way that is honest and undeniable. "The Body Key" presents strategies such as conscious breathing, mindful transitioning with movement, revisioning pain, harnessing visualized healing, and sensing the body moment to moment. The core "sense-abilities" explored in this section are literally life changing when faithfully practiced. They help move you beyond anxiety, worry, rumination, judgment, blame, shame, and fear — into the opening of possibility and flexibility that exist in the here and now.

Part 3, "The Spirit Key," taps into our inborn ability to find deep meaning and spiritual connection. Mindfulness is uniquely suited to guide us into an appreciation of the deep mystery and beauty of both inner consciousness and the outer natural world. The strategies in this section will enhance your awareness of the mythic symbols that are already present in your life, inspiring you to reconnect with and marvel at the wild places already all around but often unnoticed. You will discover the power of slowing down, using vibration and word to stimulate your spiritual awareness, and releasing your unlimited creative potential. This key addresses the fear of emptiness, lack of meaning, and creative blockage by nurturing life-affirming insights and wisdom.

Part 4, "The Relationship Key," offers down-to-earth strategies for building and enhancing relationships that are meaningful and long-lasting. Most fundamentally, life is relational and experiential. Science now understands that genes are turned on and off by their environment. Healthy relationships offer hope and support and bring us closer to realizing our potential as members of a community working together to reduce suffering and ignorance. The communal and social aspects of mindfulness are vital because they help each of us to become more attuned to justice, compassion, and diversity. You will learn strategies for overcoming loneliness, expanding empathy, extending openness to others, and forgiving past misdeeds in order to start trusting and living again.

I have to warn you, though, that you may be significantly happier after you've unlocked the code of mindfulness. You may be less worried about what is in the news and even less concerned about watching the news. You may be more inclined to stash your cell phone, reduce your texting, and spend more time building face-to-face relationships with the people you care about. You may actually stop to smell the roses outside your door, to listen to the chirping birds, or to have a meaningful conversation with someone new.

Perhaps you're already thinking, *You've got to be kidding. I don't have enough time to finish my work, and now you're going to have me stop to smell the flowers? Who has all day to talk to their partner, kids, or friends — and I'm not sure I really want to anyway because they're as stressed out as I am! As far as the news goes, I need to watch it because my business depends on it. Besides, I like texting and surfing the web on my phone. In fact, I'm getting stressed out just thinking about all these strategies for mindfulness!*

I'd be surprised if you didn't get anxious when thinking about changing your life habits. Such a response is quite normal, and I've heard it from hundreds of people I have worked with — from the healthcare professionals I train in workshops to the clients I work with individually in my office. I've also

heard how much more energized, productive, and deeply fulfilled people feel *after* they've brought mindful changes into
their lives.

Let's set aside the concern that mindfulness will turn you
into a slacker or force you to junk your computer and other
high-tech gear, because the greater awareness you acquire,
the greater the range of choices you also possess. These are
purposeful and intentional choices based on reconnecting with
your own humanity and individuality — not choices based
on the whims, desires, and intentions of others, such as cor-
porations. I know many hardworking people who use mindfulness to help them get through their busy days in more
fulfilling, joyful, compassionate, and creative ways. You will
always be in control as you decide what boundaries are necessary for living a sensible and a balanced life — even if you
choose to use the latest technology. What matters is that it will
be your choice.

Throughout *The Mindfulness Code*, I share stories to inspire and to provoke thought and reflection. Reflection and contemplation are important because they represent another aspect
of mindfulness that enriches us by inviting purpose and meaning. I remember working with a client, Steven (all clients' names
have been changed), who was fired from his stressful job because
of his anger. As Steven explained to me during our first session,
he had a difficult time not blurting out his thoughts, especially
when he was upset or felt criticized. After practicing mindfulness
over a period of several weeks — and he put in a tremendous
amount of effort — Steven came to my office and began to
share stories of how mindfulness practice had transformed his

typically negative responses into positive ones. For the first time in his life, he felt free to choose how to act. He gained a broader perspective of his previous job and angry outbursts, and he felt more in charge of his emotions. Steven committed himself to overcoming limiting thoughts in other areas as well. Having switched off his automatic reactions, he dramatically improved his relationships with his wife and others and began seeking a more meaningful career.

Intentionally Centering Attention Now is not a miracle cure, nor is it anything external that is acting upon you. Rather, it is a returning to your senses. It is a way of coming back home to the powerful tools of awareness that are our birthright; each of us is born with a perfectly designed sense-ability for being fully present. Just watch a toddler, and you will see how even the most ordinary event can bring awe-inspiring joy. Mindfulness reawakens the joyful you by rewiring habitual thoughts and beliefs that numb, censor, block, or inhibit.

Even if your life is speeding along at 110 miles per hour or you feel lost or helpless or stuck, the joyful you awaits within. Think of mindfulness as a master skill that touches your deep, genuine self, the self that understands what matters most. That self is waiting for you and has never given up on you. Slow down to use the strategies in this book and you will find that self as radiant, spacious, and calm as ever.

I hope this book will bring a few grains of peace, greater awareness, compassion, and hope into your day and our world. May we all make this journey toward a more fully awakened and mindful existence together — step by step, moment by moment.

Notes

1. APA Task Force, "Sexualization of Girls Is Linked to Common Mental Health Problems in Girls and Women — Eating Disorders, Low Self-Esteem, and Depression," www.apa.org/pi/wpo/sexualization.html (accessed February 19, 2007).
2. Balangoda Ananda Maitreya, *The Dhammapada* (Berkeley: Parallax Press, 1995), p. 1.

PART ONE

THE MIND KEY

WELCOME TO A SET OF TEACHINGS that unwrap the mind's veil to reveal the clarity within. This clarity is the code with which the mind pierces ignorance and delusion. As you approach the mind key teachings, let go of expectations. Your fresh awareness and openness is a good place to start this work.

1. Accept This Moment

The trouble with ordinary reality is that a lot of it is dull,
so we long ago decided to leave for somewhere better.

— CHARLES TART

*D*O YOU REMEMBER THE LAST TIME that you did not want to be where you were? How often have you rejected this moment with the idea that being elsewhere was far better and more fulfilling? Maybe you did not want to sit in another tiresome meeting, so your mind wandered to your weekend plans. Maybe you were relaxing by the beach on a long-needed vacation, and you suddenly thought that the view would be better from the deck of the hotel. So, you packed up your sunscreen, towels, and sunglasses, only to decide that the deck was too noisy or cold, and so you moved yet again. Or maybe you were at a party talking with someone and wished you were somewhere else with someone else. Maybe it's happening right now as you read this sentence — I won't take it personally, because I've been there myself.

On a spring day, when the sun finally breaks through the clouds, I long to go outside for a short mindfulness walk after seeing clients all morning. I sense I need to do this because I am not feeling centered and am struggling to calm my mind and stay present. My chance comes when a client calls to cancel an afternoon appointment. It is a downhill walk and only a few blocks from my office to the tall, spindly cottonwoods that line the banks of the Willamette River. The dark blue-green water is high and running fast, scattering wisps of whitecaps from one river edge to the other. A nearby green field looks like the perfect place to walk mindfully. And so I begin.

I take a couple of deep breaths, then set the intention to take my first step. I move my right leg up and forward, but before my heel touches down, my mind is already filled up, thinking of a previous interaction with a client that morning. Again, I set another intention to take a step with my left leg. Barely has it lifted when I notice that the air is cold. *This is uncomfortable*, I think and add, *I should have brought a light jacket.*

And so it goes. For the first five minutes, my unsettled mind keeps interrupting. I set an intention for each step, trying to block my active mind. *Lift the foot, move it forward, set it down, shift the weight*, I instruct my body. But it's not working. Every little sound or sight grabs my senses. My head fills with conversations that have not yet occurred and of things not yet done.

At one moment, I hear a fleeting thought. So sly and fleeting is it, in fact, that there was a time I wouldn't have even caught it; I would have just mindlessly followed its command like a subject in a deep hypnotic trance. *Go back to the office and meditate there*, it whispers seductively. *That will be better, and you'll be less distracted.*

My body stops in its tracks and almost follows the command, when suddenly the words crystallize into my awareness. Motionless, I stand on the grassy field and start to laugh and laugh. *Oh, so this walking meditation is not good enough,* I muse inwardly. *I guess I need to reject it for something better, warmer, more comfortable, and less distracting!*

At that instant there is a knowing that this is the *suchness* of my life. Suchness is touching the truth of things — that this is it. This is all there is. This is the only moment I have, for there is no other. This suchness snaps me awake like a jolt of electricity that surges and suddenly illuminates that which, only moments before, was veiled in darkness.

I start to walk again, this time with full presence and total acceptance of what is here before me: each unique blade of grass, the cool breeze brushing gently against my cheeks, the burst of laughter from children at a nearby park rising and falling on my ears like a musical jingle. I notice how each step I take on the uneven ground pulls me in a different direction. I am touched by the truth of how each of us walks our own uneven path. The inner recognition that I am walking my authentic path — regardless of its pain and struggle — somehow comforts me and lets me come to rest with the uncertainty of this journey. There is a sense that my path is enough. It doesn't need to be more or less. It doesn't need to be anywhere else.

For the next twenty minutes of mindful walking, time and space melt away. It is just me, the grass, the wind, the cottonwoods, and the river. It is peace. When I return to my office, I am ready to listen. I am ready to accept being here and nowhere else. This acceptance, however, is not resignation. Acceptance in this context does not mean giving up or resigning to a sadness, a depression, an addiction, a dead-end job, or whatever the present-moment condition may be. Rather, it is a liberating acceptance, which allows you to witness the truth and beauty of this moment — whatever label (good, bad, pleasant, unpleasant) one puts on it. So, the next time you reject the moment, consider what it is you are running from and why you are running. Perhaps it is not that reality is deadening, uninviting, stupid, unfair, or dull, but that the mind needs sharpening. An open awareness of the moment is the razor's edge you possess and can begin to use right now. This awareness takes time to cultivate, so don't give up. You can begin with the following easy practice.

The next time you feel impatient or ill at ease, pause right where you are and don't be so quick to run off to something else. Instead, simply notice whatever feelings (perhaps frustration, impatience, boredom) or thoughts precede your rejection or denial of a situation. You might ask yourself, "What is this that I'm experiencing?" See if you can accept each moment for what it is. This means not that you have to avoid judging, which is almost impossible, but that you notice your judging. To do this, even for a moment, is to sharpen your awareness and nurture a willingness to accept what is present in your life. How wondrous!

Note

Epigraph. Charles Tart, *Living the Mindful Life* (Boston: Shambhala, 1994), p. 41.

2. Wake Up from Dreams of Fantasy

Delusions are inexhaustible: I vow to transcend them.

— BODHISATTVA VOW

MCDONALD'S WILL NEVER SERVE as many burgers each day as there are fantasies being served on a planet with more than 6 billion people. The object of any single fantasy typically stirs up feelings, cravings, desires, and delusions that push and pull at us. Fantasies essentially distract us and steal away precious time that could be spent in the actual here and now. To believe that grasping for a fantasy will help you escape pain is yet another fantasy.

The Sanskrit word *bodhisattva* can be translated as "awakening being"; it refers to one who fearlessly vows to seek enlightenment to reduce suffering in the world. You don't need to be a bodhisattva to want to awaken from the many causes of suffering, such as delusion, ignorance, fantasy, selfishness, greed, envy, jealousy, and hatred. However, waking up is

difficult when there are so many fantasies to which we can easily retreat. Escapism takes many forms, and fantasy can be a
dangerous, even life-threatening, form of denial. Just knowing
this is a good place to start.

Today I am facilitating a group of nine patients with eating disorders at a clinic of Providence St. Vincent Hospital in Portland, Oregon. They are adolescent girls and young women
diagnosed with anorexia nervosa or bulimia nervosa, conditions so dangerous that the National Institute of Mental Health
reports anorexics have a mortality rate "12 times higher than
the annual death rate due to all causes of death among females
ages 15–24 in the general population."[1] After only a few minutes, it is clear my group is distracted and struggling. When I
ask what's going on, they report feeling miserable because they
are "stuck in eating-disorder thoughts." So I suggest that we
do something different: have an entirely new experience of the
room we are in. Many protest that they already know the room
inside out (or at least, they *think* they do). After a short discussion, they finally agree to give this a chance and to approach
the experience with an open and curious mind. What they don't
know is that they are about to try a mindfulness exercise that's
designed to anchor them in the present moment.

We start by taking a few calm breaths together. Then, for
the next fifteen minutes, I guide them around the room. My
instructions include having them pay extremely close attention to every little detail — such as the hairline cracks on the
floor, the shapes of chair and table legs, and little variations of
color on walls, doors, and notebooks. I ask them to notice each

movement of their feet and arms as they walk. They listen to the moment-by-moment sounds occurring inside and outside the room, as well as the sounds of their own breathing, movements, and footsteps. At one point, I have them shut their eyes as they hand a familiar object (such as a key, a pen, a notebook, or a purse) to another person, who will sense its weight, its coolness or warmth, and its hardness or softness. The room is steeped in quiet as they move about in this deliberately stealthy and purposeful manner.

When I finally ask them to return to their seats, the first thing that surprises them is how much time has passed. After we've settled in, I ask them a deceptively simple question, Where were your eating-disorder thoughts during the past fifteen minutes? Silence and an expression of shock and amazement on many of the girls' faces answer me. Not one person fiddles with a notebook or doodles on a piece of paper — a common occurrence. Their sense of awareness and presence is so strong that it seems to me as if the entire group has awakened from a trance.

After a few moments, one young girl raises her hand with an epiphany of sorts. "For the first time, I feel like my eating-disorder thoughts are a dream world or a fantasy. I feel like for a while I left that world for the real one," she says. Another girl raises her hand and comments, "I suddenly realize that I've been living in the dream world of my eating disorder and that I don't like when it gets interrupted." Others echo a similar story of irritation and unease when the fantasy is interrupted. For a brief moment, this represents a victory for these girls — many of whom live in a world where distorted thoughts and emotions regarding their body image and rigid beliefs about food and eating steal away the precious hours and days of their lives. Anorexic and bulimic fantasies are difficult to pierce, but today's group exercise brings the hope that anyone can break free of debilitating automatic behaviors, thoughts, and addictions, if only for a few moments. Today, these girls have directly experienced that possibility.

Although it is true that fantasy can sometimes serve a creative and helpful purpose, fantasy can also be an escape that blocks us from being present and living fully. What daily or weekly fantasies inhabit your mental space? How do you respond when your fantasies are interrupted? Trying to catch your mind in fantasy mode might make you angry or upset. Maybe the sheer number and type of delusions that your mind is capable of creating fascinates you. Awakening to our fantasies takes time, so be patient with the following mindfulness strategy for piercing the bubble of fantasy and participating in the present moment.

Take one day to track your fantasies by counting them and noting their content. When you notice a fantasy, you can return to the present moment by turning your mind's attention toward your surroundings, its colors, shapes, sounds, smells, and sensations. If driving, for example, you can feel your hands on the steering wheel, notice the weather, and listen to the sound of the tires on the pavement. If you find that you get upset, judgmental, or self-blaming because of your fantasies, remind yourself that a fantasy, or any thought, is not necessarily a fact. (Just because you think you're a pink elephant doesn't make it true — at least let's hope not!)

By paying attention in this way, you will learn more about your mind and yourself, as well as gently remind yourself to be more present.

Notes

Epigraph. Lama Surya Das, *Awakening the Buddha Within* (New York: Broadway Books, 1997), p. 143.

1.   The National Institute of Mental Health, "The Numbers Count: Mental Disorders in America," http://www.nimh.nih.gov/health/publica tions/the-numbers-count-mental-disorders-in-america/index.shtml (accessed December 30, 2009).

3. Create Space from Your Ego-Dominated Self

Oh, I don't inhale.

— WILLIAM STAFFORD,
when asked how he dealt with adulation and celebrity

*W*HY DO HUMAN BEINGS SUFFER and cause suffering in ways that other forms of life don't seem to? At times, it appears we are destined to be the most dramatic soap opera in the universe. If there were an interstellar television series called *Earth: The Reality Show*, it would likely command huge ratings throughout the Milky Way and beyond. But perhaps this need not be our destiny.

Whether you call it the ego (as Freud did), the pain body (as Eckhart Tolle does), or the self (as Buddhists continue to), there is a part of human awareness whose job it is to create a sense of self that is distinct and separate from others. The human brain, after all, is designed to construct an identity. Various areas of the brain are implicated in this capacity to create a solid self. The brain's left hemisphere is especially good at this, making mental road maps and cobbling together stories about our lives. It does the heavy lifting in supporting the concept of self, or I, with which we strongly identify. Harvard-trained neuroanatomist Jill Bolte Taylor describes the direct experience of losing this individuated self because of a hemorrhage in her brain's left hemisphere in her book *My Stroke of Insight: A Brain Scientist's Personal Journey*. The experience helped her understand what happens when the left brain's divisive, me-first sense of I stops totally dominating one's reality. According to Taylor, left-brain dominance produces "extremely rigid thinking patterns that are analytically critical (extreme left brain). Creating a healthy balance between our two characters enables us the ability to remain cognitively flexible enough to welcome change (right hemisphere), and yet remain concrete enough to stay a path (left hemisphere)."[1]

I'm not saying we don't need a separate ego-self to get our needs met and exist in the world. In the interest of full disclosure, I admit that my mother still tells me I am special, and I do appreciate her sentiment. Indeed, from a mother's point of view, she most certainly gives birth to a special self, and she gives a name to that self, who has an "I-dentity" with a capital *I*. Nonetheless, we can balance our I-centric awareness with a more expansive and mindful awareness, which holds the promise for greater contentment, happiness, and enthusiastic living. These different forms of awareness do not need to be exclusive of one another; they can be integrated to offer us both greater inner peace and a healthier sense of our place in the world. (See chapter 10, "Open to Your True Nature," to explore using a decentralized narrative that does not attach to the I-me-my-mine perspective.)

Now that scientists can peer into the brain with sophisticated brain-imaging devices such as a functional magnetic resonance imaging machine (fMRI), there is new information on how mindful awareness affects the brain. Even some of the Dalai Lama's monks have been rolled into giant, donut-shaped fMRIs. According to Dr. Richard Davidson, director of the Laboratory for Affective Neuroscience at the University of Wisconsin, where such brain and mindfulness studies are conducted, these monks may be the most peaceful and happy persons in the entire world. They weren't born this way, though. Through their systematic practice of meditating on compassion, they have mastered a means of creating space from their reactive, ego-dominated selves. "Anyone who says meditation is relaxation doesn't know what they're talking about. It's like trying to change the course of a river," says Davidson, who himself underwent intensive meditation practice in India.[2]

Davidson's work has helped to identify the brain circuits that stimulate feelings of happiness, contentment, and well-being. He has also shown that happiness can be learned. Research indicates that the left prefrontal cortex — the area of the brain located behind the left forehead — is highly active when one experiences positive feelings such as peacefulness, calmness, optimism, and happiness. This is not, however, the kind of self-centered hedonic happiness that brings only temporary relief from life's woes and worries. What is produced is a more enduring sense of well-being that goes beyond a short-lived positive feeling. Those who train their brains to produce positive emotions also naturally act in kind and compassionate ways. "They are poised to jump into action and do whatever they can to help relieve suffering," observes Davidson.[3] In other words, happiness and compassion are acquired skills that stimulate compassionate behavior. Davidson's work and that of other neuroscientists is substantiating what mystics and poets have taught all along about our untapped human potential.

With enough practice, one can actually transform oneself into a human being dedicated to peace and kindness without needing to wave a peace banner in another's face — which may serve only to create a fresh conflict. This is perhaps the next great revolution and evolution of the human mind. The ability to profoundly change from the inside out really does exist. Methods of training the mind for compassion and peace offer the hope that life can be experienced in a vastly more loving and caring way than it usually is on our blue planet. Just knowing that such potential exists is the beginning of turning toward happiness and rewiring your brain.

There are many contemplative, inside-out ways to turn on the mind's inner peace circuits. In addition to learning from films such as *What the Bleep Do We Know!?* or books such as Jill Bolte Taylor's *My Stroke of Insight* or Matthieu Ricard's *Happiness*, here is a useful strategy for rewiring your life with new possibility.

You don't need a mystical experience to change the brain. This week, make a point of seeking out others who have changed their lives and have become happier, less judgmental, and more tolerant of themselves and others. If you don't know of anyone, ask around until you find such a story. (You can always read chapter 25, "Awaken the Tender

Heart," which provides an example of someone who transformed his life and made a difference while doing so.) Sometimes, we just need to hear what is possible from a supportive, caring, and empathetic person in order for our brains to start making changes.

Notes

Epigraph. Jeff Baker, "Oregon Poet William Stafford Still Popular — 15 Years after His Death," *The Oregonian*, Sunday, July 6, 2008, www .oregonlive.com/news/oregonian/index.ssf?/base/news/1215226 518277170.xml&coll=7 (accessed June 2009).

1.   Jill Bolte Taylor, *My Stroke of Insight: A Brain Scientist's Personal Journey* (New York: Viking Press, 2007), p. 138.

2.   Penelope Green, "This Is Your Brain on Happiness," *O, the Oprah Magazine*, March 2008, www.oprah.com/article/omagazine/200803 _omag_happiness (accessed June 2009).

3.   Ibid.

4. Observe Your Mind

What lies behind us
And what lies before us
Are tiny matters
Compared to what lies within us.

— ANONYMOUS

*I*f YOU TRULY WANT TO CHANGE YOUR LIFE, you must first be willing to change your mind. This requires using the mind to look inward and observe its own workings. What is it attracted to, repelled by, confused by, or put to sleep by? Such inquiry is possible because our mind is the single greatest tool of observation, discrimination, and awareness that exists. All of humankind's greatest scientific discoveries are created by mind, observed by mind, and interpreted by mind. In the process of observing your own mind, you embark on the greatest inside job ever: using the mind to look in upon itself.

Watching the mind is a natural ability we all possess and one of the reasons that the mind key is possible at all. The ability to pay attention to where your mind is at any one moment is the basis for Buddhist psychology, which has a 2,500-year history of examining the mind. Brain science is adding new wrinkles by

describing which brain areas are active when we pay attention.
Buddhists, modern scientists, and psychologists know that paying attention to anything — be it your own mind or something
external — takes energy. If you are going to observe your mind,
you need effort and energy to sustain the attention required.

When I first meet Carrie, she seems quite literally to be a bundle of nerves. Although she is a tall and attractive woman in
her late thirties, her pale complexion, sunken cheeks, limp
brown hair, and clenched jaw make her appear several years
older. Shaking Carrie's hand, I notice how cold it is, and though
it is fairly warm outside, she is layered up in a blouse, a sweater,
and a knitted scarf. All that's missing are the gloves. My mind
observes these facts and files away the thought to follow up with
questions about a possible eating disorder.

Moments after sitting on a flower-patterned sofa, she fidg-
ets and blurts out, "My life is very complicated. To tell the
truth, it's a complete mess." As I hear Carrie's story, I can understand why she is upset. A single mother of two children,
she has already endured a messy divorce from a husband who
cheated on her and with whom she is still emotionally entangled. She works a full-time job and can't say "no" to any assignment that comes along for fear of being judged incompetent
or low achieving. In addition, Carrie explains that she is now
dating another man who is abusive to her. She feels so driven
by her negative emotions of anger, frustration, fear, and sadness
that she is unable to make healthier life choices. As far as Carrie
is concerned, she *is* her emotions.

As I work with Carrie over time, I discover that she has a

history of eating-disordered behavior, mostly anorexia, which she is able to control except under extreme duress. Although she has a habit of skipping meals, Carrie agrees to commit to eating protein (string cheese, a hard-boiled egg, almonds, soy milk, or some other protein-based food) throughout the day because protein helps the frontal lobe of the brain work more effectively. Carrie's inner limbic system — the reactive and stress-producing part of her brain — has been working overtime. Carrie, like all of us, needs to activate the frontal cortex, the analyzing, judging, planning, and decision-making part of the brain.

I also work with Carrie to activate the part of her mindful brain that focuses on attention and observation. The part of the brain that can note its inner workings — as if from a distance, in a neutral and nonjudgmental way — is the prefrontal and orbital frontal cortex, located behind the forehead and eyes. Thought experiments (much like those Einstein used) can help to stimulate this part of the brain. Here is one such thought experiment, which I would like you to try for yourself.

Imagine you are in line at the store, and you see a friend with whom you haven't spoken in some time. This person has just checked out and is walking toward the exit. You wave and call his or her name, but still this friend leaves the store without turning around. What do you think and feel when this happens? How might this affect your behavior toward this friend?

The objective here is to start paying closer attention to how your mind makes contact with an event or an object, how it then interprets and responds with a related emotion, and finally, how that emotion produces a behavior or an action. For example, if you interpret your friend as snubbing or ignoring you, then you may feel hurt or angry. A possible behavior resulting from that interpretation might be that you no longer contact this friend. However, if your interpretation is that your friend is going through a hard time and was lost in his or her own thoughts, you may feel sad or concerned and decide to follow up with a call as soon as you get home. The point here is that different minds make different interpretations and evaluations of everyday events. By paying close attention to how our brain makes decisions, we can notice hidden patterns and habits and even decide to test an interpretation before absorbing a powerful emotion.

My work with Carrie continues to focus on helping her to activate and strengthen the observational and attention-oriented parts of her brain. Up for the challenge, she completes all the assignments I give her. Then one day, Carrie comes in and sits down, with a confidence and a calmness flickering in her eyes. She shares a story about her ex-husband. Past encounters with him have thrown her off balance and into fits of uncontrollable anger and binge drinking, but when she spoke with him most recently, she was able to respond in an entirely different way. "For the first time in my life, I found I could control my emotions with my thoughts. I didn't think that it was possible," she says proudly and with a rare smile. Carrie's new-found strength comes from her finding new interpretations and accepting frustration, not from losing control and using alcohol to numb her feelings.

The Mind Key 35

Learning new behaviors doesn't happen overnight. Observing the mind takes time and effort. By using any of the mind key teachings, you will be accessing and strengthening new brain pathways. The purpose of this particular teaching is to focus more directly on sustaining attention. It's easy to lose focus and awareness, which is why I prefer to call mindfulness "re-mindfulness."

Attention is critical because it is always present when we observe anything. The more tasks we perform simultaneously, the more we reduce the mind's ability to sustain attention on any one thing, especially our awareness of the mind itself. This may not seem important, unless you feel overwhelmed by stress, can't sleep at night because your mind races like a supersonic plane, or can't focus on your work for any length of time. What follows is an excellent method for energizing the attentional circuitry of the brain. This attention practice is doubly useful because it also uses the breath. You can practice it anywhere you happen to be. It's totally portable, and no one will ever know you are using it. Before practicing this, I suggest you read chapter 12, the body key teaching titled "Breathe Consciously and Mindfully" (page 79).

We will combine two very important mind-and-body teachings. Here's how it works. You are going to pay attention to each breath you take. For each inbreath and outbreath, you will count, starting at one and continuing until you have reached the number twenty-five — meaning you will take twenty-five breaths.

The idea here is to keep the mind sharp and attentive while breathing. When I was in the monastery, I learned to count with rosary beads to improve the skills of focus, attention, and concentration. The rosary has 108 beads on it. If I reached the end and only counted 107, I knew I had lost attention somewhere along the way. If you find that you have lost your count, just begin again with number one. You can also observe the thoughts and the emotions that arise when you've lost concentration. Notice these thoughts with a sense of neutrality, as if they are passing clouds. Let them go and begin counting again. You may notice that when you are tired or sleepy, you don't have the same concentration power. Don't worry if you can't get to twenty-five right off the bat. Practice for five to ten minutes a day until you do reach twenty-five. Then aim for fifty!

Here is one more useful strategy for observing your mind by Intentionally Centering Attention Now.

Keep a Top-Ten-Negative-Thoughts Journal, and list in it the negative thoughts rattling around in your head. You may not always be aware of these thoughts or even how frequently they appear. Notice what themes they have in common, such as blaming or criticizing. Do this for at least a week, knowing that your thoughts do not define you. This practice increases the ability to observe thoughts in a more calm and neutral way, without letting them push you around.

5. Do One Joyful Thing Right Now

In my own hands I hold a bowl of tea;
I see all of nature represented in its green color.
Closing my eyes I find green mountains
and pure water within my own heart.
Silently sitting alone and drinking tea,
I feel these become part of me.

— SOSHITSU SEN XV

*W*HY IS IT THAT THERE NEVER SEEMS TO BE ENOUGH TIME? We always seem to be short of time, trying to cram more into each moment. We buy timesaving devices, which promise to shave seconds off each task, so we can more quickly move on to the next task — and the next. It's as if we're never quite satisfied to stay in one place too long because time is passing, and the only way to cure this illusion of lost time is to speed up and do more. Even the cosmetic and beauty industries promise to help our bodies turn back time.

Fortunately, our language provides a vast array of words that describe how to set aside time for better time management, such as work time, vacation time, family time, quality time (which implies nonquality time), playtime, sick time, coffee time, break time, lunchtime, dinner time, exercise or workout time, and time to party. What seems to suffer most in the effort to get the most out of our lifetime is our sleep time.

Suppose, however, you woke up this morning to learn about a startling new scientific finding. The headline — heralded on television, in blogs, twitters, and the *New York Times* — is "Scientists Discover Time Does Not Exist!" This would be the equivalent of discovering that the world is round, not flat. Imagine the shift in consciousness when people realized they wouldn't fall off the edge of the earth upon reaching the horizon! And yet, we live as if the world of time is flat and linear.

Could you live without time? Some cultures do not even have words for "future" or "past." I'm saying not that there's no place for planning or preparation but that we are overly preoccupied with time-think. What if time were round, plump, squeezable, and all right here, not a shred to be found before or after? Can you imagine what that would be like?

Dawn has barely broken this morning when I step out of the house with a solitary goal in mind: to get *The Oregonian*, deposited each morning in an oblong, yellow container that stands next to the mailbox. This morning I am in a hurry, and my mind churns with I-centric thoughts of future time. *What should I eat for breakfast? I need to return those calls from yesterday. What handouts do I need to print for that next class? I wonder how many clients I am seeing today. I'm running late, so I'd better hurry. . . .*

Halfway down the long driveway, a jolting awareness suddenly breaks into this stream of thoughts. I stop in my tracks. The message is clear and direct: *I'm not really here, not really present*. It's true. Like the characters in the television series *Lost*, I am marooned and separated from what I most long for: a connection to what is true, real, and meaningful. I have drifted off to planning and musing about the next thing. This is a time- and outcome-based approach, one driven, at least to some extent, by the desire to determine and control the future. But where does it get me when I'm walking to pick up the newspaper? Does it really add anything?

And so, instead of walking to get the morning newspaper, I walk simply in order to walk. The effect is rather like being blind one moment and then looking through a telescope that magnifies not only sight but also sound and all other senses. In the blink of an eye, it all changes, and I am no longer alone. Walking to walk, I notice the towering fir trees, the chilly morning air, the brown pinecones on the ground, the warble of a red-headed finch darting across my path, the gurgling of a fountain, my own pulsing body, muscles contracting and loosening in my legs and arms with each small step. All catapult me into the undeniable aliveness of the moment. As I walk simply to walk, each breath fills my lungs with crisp, invigorating air. The demands of time and things not yet done have fallen away, and this is what remains. I've suddenly returned to the present, where time is endless and everlasting.

It probably takes me a good ten minutes to get the paper and return to the house (so much for being in a hurry!). But there is a new view in my eyes, my mind, and my heart. For a few moments, I have simply followed the path described by Abraham Joshua Heschel in his book *The Sabbath*, in which he describes the Sabbath as a sacred time that occurs when one stops being the artist, painter, and creator of the world's canvas, pausing instead to put the easel aside and simply *be in the world*. Heschel says, "To observe the Sabbath is to celebrate the coronation of a day in the spiritual wonderland of time."[1] Each of us has the capability to enter this holy wonderland by fully entering the present. Many paradigm shifts have been written about, but perhaps none is more attainable and nourishing than shifting from endless mind-tripping to doing one thing — walking, eating, sitting, standing, reading — with total presence, ease, and joy.

Many retail stores now utilize what are known as performance monitoring systems to speed up the checkout process by timing each transaction. Some cashiers who work under such systems are actually afraid to do anything that might slow them down, such as smiling or talking with customers. If you also feel as though you are a slave to time and efficiency, you can always enter the present moment — which is beyond time — by making use of the strategy that follows.

When was the last time you completely dedicated and devoted yourself to the experience you were having with another person? Bring your full attention to deeply notice another person today — the color of his eyes or the gentle curvature of her forehead, the way the hair falls, the unique sound and tone of the voice, the shape of the hand and fingers, and even the deeper need for well-being and happiness.

Know that this person is the most important person in your life in this moment, for as Tolstoy writes in his short story "Three Questions": "The most necessary [individual] is he with whom you are, for no man knows whether he will ever have dealings with any one else."[2] This practice not only brings you into the present but also honors the uniqueness that exists in each being. Let this meeting with another be the most important thing in your life, just for the few moments or minutes that it lasts. Could you live each moment of your day this way? How beautiful!

Notes

Epigraph. Soshitsu Sen XV, *Tea Life, Tea Mind* (New York and Tokyo: Weatherhill, 1995), p. 81.

1. Abraham Joshua Heschel, *The Sabbath* (New York: Farrar, Strauss, and Giroux, 1996), p. 18.

2. Leo Tolstoy, "Three Questions," in Amy Kass, ed., *Giving Well, Doing Good: Readings for Thoughtful Philanthropists* (Bloomington, IN: Indiana University Press, 2007), p. 242.

6. Use Sacred Word to Turn Away from Despair

In the beginning was the Word,
and the Word was with God, and the Word was God.

— JOHN I:I

In the beginning was Brahman, with whom was the Word;
and the Word was truly the supreme Brahman.

— RIG VEDA

In the beginning, the Word gave the Father his origin.

— HUITOTO INDIANS

*I*N THE BEGINNING WAS THE WORD." This is a simple yet
revealing sentence, filled with layers upon layers of meaning. It echoes throughout the cosmology of diverse religious
traditions and hints at both the unknown mysteries of the universe and the origin of its creation. It captures our collective
imagination, bringing us to the edge of truth and knowing. But
mostly, it asks us to look deeper into the mystery, essence, and
connection between sound and our lives.

The practice of using sound and *mantra*, or sacred word,
has been around for thousands of years. In Hindu literature,
the earliest Vedic hymns give mantra a legacy dating from
1500 BCE. The recitation of these hymns by Hindu priests probably adds another two thousand years of oral history to spiritual practices using sound, word, and music. Word, vibration,
and thought, whether we are listening to a chant or reciting a

blessing before mealtime, hold the potential to transform our lives and enliven our spirit. The words you choose to place your attention on also determine the well-being of the inner circuitry of your brain and the outer circuitry of your life.

The sun is shining brightly on this spectacular summer afternoon. I was outside hours earlier, but now I lie in bed in excruciating pain after returning from the hospital. In an act of loving-kindness gone awry (the best term for it), my own cat bit me and caused me to fall when I rescued it from two large and rather menacing dogs. The realization that I'm going to spend the next two months in a wheelchair and another four months on crutches sinks in. *I'm going to miss out on enjoying the whole summer. Why didn't I let my cat calm down before trying to move it away from the fence? That was really, really stupid of me. Now look where I am*, says my turbulent mind, making me feel as though I am about to go rafting on whitewater without a life jacket.

In that moment, I notice these blaming thoughts as if from a distance. *Stop!* I think to myself in the mental equivalent of a shout. This blocks the negative thoughts for a moment. I do this because I understand that while intense pain — such as that caused by my injured hip — is an inevitable part of life, suffering is optional. When the negative thoughts start up again, I ask myself these questions: *Do I really want to add this suffering to my life? Will it help me heal any faster? Will it make me feel any happier?* Knowing that I need to regulate and calm my emotions quickly, I instantly draw upon an ancient form of I-CAN, or Intentionally Centering Attention Now.

I start by focusing on my breath and mentally intoning, *May all beings be safe, happy, healthy, and at peace. May I be safe, happy, healthy, and at peace.* When my thoughts stray, I gently bring them back. All the while, I breathe diaphragmatically, being present and in my body — even in my injured hip. Within minutes, I sense a greater calm and spaciousness within myself as I fully accept this present-moment condition (although this doesn't mean I prefer it!). *At least,* says a compassionate and slightly humorous inner voice, *you will know how to do things differently if the cat situation should happen again. But this is the way it is right now.*

Do the words we choose really make that big a difference in our daily lives? Can they change our reality? Can they help us heal, physically and mentally? Dr. Larry Dossey, author of *Healing Words* and *Prayer Is Good Medicine*, has written extensively about what he believes is a well-documented but underrated means of healing. In an interview, Dossey says, "Meditation is a powerful way of entering into healing states. [Research] ... has shown that meditative states, and almost any kind of contemplative state, can be good for the body.... For example, at the University of California San Francisco Medical School, they actually tested healing intentions, which were initiated at a great distance by several individuals, for people with advanced AIDS. This was a double-blind study. The people who received the healing intentions statistically did much better than people who did not. So this is not just fantasy. This is a valid phenomenon, which has been tested."[1]

New evidence, published in 2008 in the peer-reviewed online journal *Current Issues in Education*, shows that Transcendental Meditation (a practice of mentally repeating a word for
a length of time) produced a 50 percent improvement in attention deficit hyperactivity disorder (ADHD) in middle-school
students who meditated twice daily — without the side effects
that can occur with drug interventions. In their conclusion, the
researchers write that "the technique has potential to improve
attention, behavior regulation, and executive function by naturally reducing stress and anxiety and improving brain functioning."[2] The noticeable reduction in stress is worth noting,
since stress disrupts the brain's ability to learn. Stress actually
dumbs down the frontal lobe, where much thinking takes place,
because stress diverts blood to the emotional core of the brain.

Christian centering prayer, the mantras of Buddhism, and
Transcendental Meditation all use a word or a phrase repeated
over and over as a means of turning away from suffering and
despair in order to locate peace. I adapted part of the loving-
kindness practice (see chapters 24 and 36) to locate peace after
my injury. The words you can use are infinite. You could, for
example, mentally repeat words or phrases such as *one*, *quiet
mind*, *peace*, or *now*. You might decide to use a prayer, such as
the Christian prayer "Lord Jesus Christ, have mercy upon me."
Feel free to be creative, using words that feel good. For example, I know an avid golfer who finds the phrase "bogey free" to
be calming and helpful for him.

Practicing I-CAN with the breath and a meaningful word
is a wonderful way to quiet the mind, quell anxiety and stress,
and build concentration. Here are a few useful guidelines for
using this strategy.

To begin, allow yourself quiet time to reflect on which word or words you want to use. If a word does not feel right, change it, or if a word triggers intrusive memories or associations, find a word that is not charged in this way. Even using a neutral word such as *one* has been shown to lower stress. Once you've chosen your word, find a quiet place to sit, indoors or outdoors. You can do this exercise lying down, but it's better to be sitting up because it will be easier to stay awake. This is true even if you are sitting up in bed. Avoid practicing for one to two hours after a meal because you may get too drowsy to stay focused.

Allow yourself at least ten minutes twice daily to practice centering your attention. Sitting quietly, close your eyes. While repeating your word, you will be placing much of your focus on the breath. Make sure you breathe evenly and into the belly. As you think of your word(s), you do not need to concentrate hard; instead, imagine that you are simply preferring or favoring your chosen word over others. If your mind goes off into thinking about the past or the future for a while, that's okay. And if you get drowsy, that's okay too. Just allow yourself to favor the word again.

Sometimes the word may feel as though it has gone inward, as though you're still with it, though not repeating it. If this happens, allow yourself to experience the word this way. Your other senses may also intrude as you repeat your word. You may hear a noise, or you may feel a sensation in your body. Don't push these away; rather, just notice them and return to the breath and the word.

This practice can sometimes bring up different thoughts and emotions. Should you feel a strong negative feeling, see what it is like to sit with it until it passes. Your mind will naturally be drawn to it. You don't need to explain or understand the feeling, but do let yourself notice if it increases or lessens in intensity. If for any reason a negative feeling lasts for a long time, you can always stop the practice by opening your eyes, lying down, or resting. Know that you can always refocus your attention on the breath during or after any strong emotional feeling. On the other hand, you may experience an uplifting feeling while doing this practice. Whatever your experience may be today, the next practice session may well bring different feelings. Give yourself permission to be open to whatever arises.

This is a gentle practice, so if you feel the need to shift your position on the ground, chair, or bed, go ahead and do so — just do so with full awareness. You may want to use a watch or a clock the first few times you try this. With more practice, you will come to sense when your ten minutes are up. Before you open your eyes at the end, allow yourself to sit in the presence of your body with compassion. Then, slowly open your eyes. You may also want to end your ten minutes of attentiveness with a short affirmation or blessing of thanks.

Notes

1. Dennis Hughes, "On the Role of Prayer and Meditation in Medicine," *Share Guide*, www.shareguide.com/Dossey.html (accessed June 27, 2009).

2. Sarina Grosswald, William Stixrud, Fred Travis, and Mark Bateh, "Use of the Transcendental Meditation Technique to Reduce Symptoms of Attention Deficit Hyperactivity Disorder (ADHD) by Reducing Stress and Anxiety: An Exploratory Study," *Current Issues in Education* 10, no. 2, http://cie.asu.edu/volume10/number2/ (accessed January 15, 2010).

7. Prime Your Mind for Trust

We do not believe in ourselves until someone reveals
that deep inside us something is valuable, worth listening to,
worthy of our trust, sacred to our touch.

— E. E. CUMMINGS

BRITISH PSYCHIATRIST JOHN BOWLBY was a pioneer in the field of child-parent bonding and attachment. He learned that from early infancy to the tender age of three, our sense of trust, safety, and well-being is greatly shaped by the relationships we have with our caregivers and the environment. When parents or caregivers are responsive to a child's needs by being communicative, emotionally confident, and available, that child develops what is known as a secure attachment style. A securely attached child is more likely to be flexible, communicative, and less reactive to the environment. This child learns that getting one's needs met is neither scary nor difficult and that communication and emotions are useful tools.

But what happens when a child cannot get her or his needs met because the parent responds in an inconsistent or unpredictable way — perhaps at times responsive but at other times anxious, upset, preoccupied, or even rejecting or abusive? In response to a harsh, stressful, or traumatic environment, children develop an insecure attachment style because they have learned that relationship and emotional needs are difficult, if not impossible, to fulfill.

Human beings' experience with caregivers at a young age wires the brain. The insecurely attached child's brain is put on high alert. The brain's emotional core, or limbic system, primes that child — and the adult it will become — to expect chaos and stress. Life is a constant struggle for such an individual, when safety and trust are neither expected nor found.

Is it possible to reverse a life history of insecure attachment? To transform deep feelings of mistrust and reactivity into feelings of openness and trust? Phillip Shaver, a distinguished professor of psychology at the University of California in Davis, and Mario Mikulincer, a professor of psychology at the Interdisciplinary Center in Herzlyia, Israel, both specialize in adult attachment and have researched how feelings of mistrust can be altered. In one study, after participants answered a questionnaire identifying their insecure relationship attachments, Shaver and Mikulincer exposed these individuals to words that indicate closeness and security, such as *love*, *caring*, and *supportive*. Attachment researchers call this technique "a security priming." In their book *Attachment in Adulthood*, Shaver and Mikulincer explain, "Using priming techniques, attachment researchers have found that momentary activation of mental representations of available and supportive attachment figures has beneficial effects on expectations of . . . [another's] . . . behavior."[1] In other words, someone experiencing a security priming is more open and trusting of others.

The Buddha actually created the first security priming more than 2,500 years ago when he taught loving-kindness practice as a means to help monks overcome their deepest fears while meditating in the jungle. What follows is a guided exercise on security priming. I have used it to help many individuals overcome anxiety, fear, or various forms of trauma, including posttraumatic stress disorder (PTSD). Use this exercise when you are having difficulty in close relationships, if you have persistent feelings of dread, worry, or anxiety, or if you have experienced trauma — whether caused by injury, accident, near loss of life, or any other life-altering experience. We've all undergone trauma in this lifetime, so this may be useful even if you can't pinpoint a specific traumatic event.

As always, find a safe and comfortable place, where you will not be disturbed, to sit. This security priming is portable, so you can use it whenever and wherever you need. Assume an upright and relaxed position. Begin by taking three satisfying breaths to ground you in the body. As you do this, notice your feet on the floor and your body on the chair.

Bring to mind a place you love — the beach, the woods, a favorite park or room — anyplace where you feel totally safe and comfortable. Once you've located that place, take a few moments to picture all the things you appreciate about it. Now breathe in the pure air of this favorite place. Let the air fill your lungs. With each new breath, imagine the joy, purity, and well-being you find in this favorite place filling all the cells of your body. Continue with these breaths until your whole body — from the tips of your toes to the top of your head — is filled with joy, purity, and well-being. You may even notice your eyes, face, and jaw relaxing. Perhaps there is a slight smile at the corners of your mouth. Settle into this relaxed state. You may want to spend a few seconds noticing your abdomen as it rises and falls with each breath.

Now you are going to use your imagination. Remember that you are always in control. If you ever feel uncomfortable, you have the option of opening your eyes and discontinuing this exercise. If you should feel overwhelmed by this exercise, you might want to seek professional guidance to help you work through the difficulty. And don't feel bad about any difficulties; instead, recognize your own wisdom telling you to get more guidance. Only go as far with this exercise as feels right for you at any one time. You don't need to experience the whole security priming all at once. Even a little bit of this practice will move you toward reclaiming a sense of inner trust and security.

Now reflect for a moment on how every person who has ever been alive — we're talking all of history — has had to deal with some kind of difficult situation. Like all these others who have faced emotional and physical pain, stress, and tribulation, you also face some difficult or problematic situation that you have not been able to resolve. This problem could be many things — a feeling such as dread, anxiety, or unworthiness; something rooted in the past, such as a difficult relationship, memory, or event, that has caused you to suffer for a long time; or perhaps a difficult situation that you are facing right now.

As you visualize this, I want you to sense where in the body you feel this difficulty. Your body stores the memory of a trauma, so it can be helpful to feel where the energy is stored so that it can be released at some point. See if it's possible to watch the energy from a safe distance, to notice it in a neutral way. How intense is it? Over what area of the body is it? Is it heavy or light? Is it hard and thick like armor or soft and thin like a bubble?

For the next part of this exercise, imagine that you are not alone as you experience this difficulty. Visualize yourself surrounded by people who are understanding about and sensitive to your anguish. They are all around you; the crowd is growing moment by moment. All have come to be close to you at this difficult time. These people could be family, friends, and others who may not know you directly but have heard about your situation and want to show their support. Even a loving pet can join to offer you love. If you have had problems with some family members and don't feel understood or supported by them, allow yourself to expand your connection to others, living or dead, who you know would care about you. This could be a compassionate grandparent or other distant relative, as well as historical figures such as Jesus, Gandhi, Mother Teresa, or anyone else you admire. There are people like that who will stand by your side right now. They lend their complete and total support. They want to be close to you, and you can even imagine them holding your hand, giving you a hug, or placing a comforting hand on your shoulder. They extend their fullest sense of love and compassion toward you. Imagine them all congregating around you to form a circle of caring, closeness, understanding, and protection.

Take several satisfying, deep breaths. With each in-breath, let yourself soak up the feeling of safety and caring these gentle people are offering you. You may notice this as a tingling or a feeling of warmth or stillness. Let yourself smile at the many kind faces all around you. And as you think about your difficult situation, know that these caring and compassionate individuals want to assist you because they genuinely care for you. They are willing to be there for you and understand what you are going through because they too have experienced hardship. Like you, all needed support at some time in their lives. More than anything, they want you to know that you are understood and that they care for your well-being. Spend the next few minutes letting your inner being be touched by the caring and safety these people offer you. They have no agenda other than to be there for you, and they are certain you have the strength and wisdom to move forward. Continue to visualize them with you.

Now focus your attention on the blessings being sent to you by all who surround you. With love and recognition of your strength, openness, and courage, they send you this blessing: "May you be safe, happy, healthy, and at peace, free from pain and suffering." Accept the support offered to you now, and feel the sense of safety, security, and protection that surrounds you as you rest in this supportive and caring circle. Spend a few minutes letting this blessing seep deep inside of you. You may even say for yourself: "May I be safe, happy, healthy, and at peace, free from pain and suffering. May my body let go of old hurts as I move forward in my life with the support and strength and love of so many." When you are ready, slowly open your eyes and reorient yourself to the room.

This inner journey takes courage, so give yourself a pat on the back. If trauma is an ongoing stressor in your life, you may want to explore books such as Peter Levine's *Waking the Tiger* and *Healing Trauma*. Here is another good strategy for priming your mind to trust.

Check in with your body's sensations when you are with others. Is it sharing an old feeling or one that is happening in the here and now? Reflect on how you can you tell the difference. Trust what your body is feeling. Remember to use the security priming whenever you need to address overwhelming feelings.

Notes

Epigraph. William Watson Purkey and Betty L. Siegel, *Becoming an Invitational Leader: A New Approach to Professional and Personal Success* (Lake Worth, FL: Humanics Trade Group, 2002), p. 152.

1. Mario Mikulincer and Phillip Shaver, *Attachment in Adulthood: Structure, Dynamics, and Change* (New York: Guilford Press, 2007), p. 67.

8. Light the Spark of Creativity

When I am working on a problem, I never think about beauty.
I think only how to solve the problem. But when I have finished,
if the solution is not beautiful, I know it is wrong.

— BUCKMINSTER FULLER

IMAGINE YOU ARE FLYING a Cessna 172 Skyhawk across Colorado's rugged Uncompahgre Plateau. You are lost in the clouds, more than six thousand feet in altitude, when your wings suddenly ice up and the engine loses 75 percent of its power. You face no other option but to drop below the clouds into a canyon. When the clouds clear, you find there is no place to land except for an isolated, rocky, and tree-strewn terrain that is rapidly approaching. Somehow you manage to land the small craft, but during the ensuing crash, the plane is destroyed. Miraculously, you crawl out of the wreck into eight-foot-high snowdrifts. With only bruises and cuts, you are lucky to be alive. But what do you do next? Can creativity save your life?

The above scenario actually happened to a relatively new pilot, 57-year-old Scott Thurner, who did not have the benefit of survival training. To make matters worse, he had failed to file a flight plan. Any number of wrong decisions from this point forward could have brought tragedy. But Thurner's creativity helped to save his life. Rather than take his modest food supply and try to climb out of the canyon to head for the small town of Montrose, located twenty miles away, he decided to stay put. Before doing anything else, Thurner dug a shallow snow cave to keep from freezing to death.

What did he use as a life-sheltering roof for what he later referred to as his Motel 6? Thurner's plane was so thrashed that the door was ripped off. Improvising, he dragged this door to his cave to help maintain his body heat. Later, he looked for the plane's beacon transmitter and found it was intact. Again, Thurner made a critical and insightful decision not to activate it that night, which would have drained the plane's battery. He waited until daytime to turn it on — a move that saved his life. He also found some red tape, which he used to form the shape of a big red *X* on one of the Cessna's wings — wings that otherwise blended in with the white snow. On the second night, Thurner dug a larger snow cave, which he dubbed his Holiday Inn. Again, he used the plane's door as a roof and turned off the transmitter to conserve energy. Amazingly, after thirty hours in a canyon so rugged that even a helicopter rescue was impossible, Thurner was found. Rescuers had to snowshoe in to save him.

Have you ever had the experience of trying to solve a difficult problem — not necessarily a life-or-death one like Thurner's — but found yourself blocked, stuck, frustrated, at a loss? And then, when you least expected it — perhaps at the time when you felt most hopeless and had given up — the solution appeared in a flash? This moment of letting go and making space for a creative answer captivates brain scientists. They want to better understand the two primary ways that the brain solves problems, either analytically or intuitively. Intuitive awareness, which can be thought of as a moment of inspiration or insight, seems to occur after periods of high stress when the analytic goal is released. During the process of relaxing and letting go, the creative *aha!* solution appears.

A wonderful example of applying intuition as a moment-by-moment life skill is found in music. After listening to a concert by jazz pianist McCoy Tyner, music reviewer Barry Johnson wrote, "Jazz makes us smarter, more creative, more adaptable. You listen to Tyner carefully, and he suggests new avenues to try in your own life. A dead end doesn't have to be fatal."[1] In life, as in jazz, how do you find new avenues when it seems you have reached a dead end? Nancy Andreasen, psychiatrist and author of *The Creating Brain*, says that creativity may "begin with a process during which associative links run wild, creating new connections, many of which might seem strange or implausible."[2] While analytical thinking uses a smaller set of brain networks, intuitive thinking basically lets the brain run wild with thoughts and ideas. In other words, entirely new connections and associations are made without censoring or limiting them. To do this, however, we need to take a risk or a leap of creative faith.

Is it possible to teach ourselves the process of letting go and arriving at novel solutions to problems? To think freely and divergently, the brain needs spaciousness to allow for new patterns of activity. Brain scientists think that the frontal cortex, located behind the forehead, acts like the director of a play or a film who brings all the elements of the production together. But to be creative, the director also needs to let go of control at some point. As Einstein said, "The intuitive mind is a sacred gift and the rational mind is a faithful servant. We have created a society that honors the servant and has forgotten the gift."[3]

Physicist and director of the Centre for the Mind at the University of Sydney, Allan Snyder has been studying and working with savants, those who possess astonishingly complex computational powers and artistic abilities. Some savants possess advanced abilities to play music or draw at very young ages; others similarly show remarkable learning and intellectual abilities. One savant, for example, became fluent in the difficult ancient Germanic language of Íslenska, or Icelandic, in just a week. Snyder believes that the processing power of savants is available to everyone. The secret, he says, is letting go of conceptualization, because often our fixed ideas block our hidden but existing capabilities. According to Snyder, "We see constellations instead of the individual stars. To be creative, you have to join the dots up in a unique way. But how can you do that if you keep superimposing the ways you already know?"[4] Snyder works with a device called a transcranial magnetic stimulator, or TMS cap, which fits over the head like a ski cap, to turn off the brain's conceptual areas and make space for its innate creative abilities.

Here is a strategy for sparking your creative insight without a TMS cap. The more you use this, the more you will rewire your brain for intuitive and divergent thought.

When stuck on a problem, give yourself permission to let go of needing to find an analytical solution. Release your expectations and do something relaxing, such as taking a walk, going to the zoo, or listening to music. When you become present with your surroundings, you help your mind quiet down from its inner noise.

Notes

Epigraph. David J. Darling, *The Universal Book of Mathematics* (New Jersey: John Wiley and Sons, 2004), p. 34.

1.   Barry Johnson, "Jazz Builds Better Brains — Really," *The Oregonian*, February 23, 2009, http://blog.oregonlive.com/portlandarts/2009/02/jazz_builds_better_brains_real.html (accessed June 2009).

2.   Bryan Appleyard, "Does Our Brain Have a Switch That Makes Everyone an Einstein?" *Dana Foundation's Brain in the News*, December 2008, p. 5 (reprinted from *London Times*, November 16, 2008).

3.   Gary F. Moring, *The Complete Idiot's Guide to Understanding Einstein* (New York: Penguin, 2004), p. 286.

4.   Douglas S. Fox, "The Inner Savant," *Discover Presents the Brain*, Winter 2009, p. 15.

9. Invite the Power and Peace of Intention

When we develop the habit of noticing our intentions,
we have a much better compass with which to navigate our lives.
We learn to cast a glance at our motivation before we speak or act,
which frees us to live the life we want.

— SHARON SALZBERG

HOW STRONG A FORCE IS INTENTION? Does setting an intention really work? If you're not sure about the power of intention, think for a moment about all the items in your household and in your life at this moment. None of this just appeared out of nowhere. An intention preceded the wanting, the buying, the getting that relationship, and more. Every action or deed begins with an intention, whether that intention is conscious or unconscious. Advertisers know this, and they set the intention to get us to buy their products. If we're not paying attention, the intentions of others can become our intentions.

Intentions can be harmful, beneficial, or neutral. Intentions are the seeds you plant to produce the eventual yield of your life. When an intention is repeated time and time again, the groove created by that intention becomes a habit or sometimes an addiction. Habit then shapes one's brain, one's character, and one's life. Problems occur when intentions are unconscious or unheeded, when we are not the master of our intentions. Intention also has a broader meaning and application that author Wayne Dyer describes as reconnecting with source and uncovering purpose. Intentions are critical because they can morph directly into our worldly actions. To identify intention is to touch the heart of mindfulness: fully awakening to the moment, unencumbered from delusion and ignorance, and affirming deepest purpose.

When I first meet Patrick, a married man in his late thirties, he tells me he is depressed because his wife wants a divorce. I ask what has led to this situation, and Patrick describes his troubling obsession with sex and the Internet. He wrings his hands as he recounts how his behavior escalated from viewing pornography to arranging meetings for sex in riskier and riskier situations.

"My wife found out, and now she wants to leave me," he says, hanging his head. "I want to keep the marriage together, but I don't know how." When I tell Patrick that his behavior reveals sexual addiction, he is shocked. After some initial denial, Patrick realizes how his actions have hurt others, and he begins to accept and work with his addiction, his habitual and unconscious intentions. This willingness to accept is itself an intention to move in a new direction, in terms of both brain pathways and life pathways.

The vigorous and ongoing scientific debate about the nature of intention has spurred brain researchers to identify an area in the prefrontal cortex of the brain that activates *before* we make a conscious choice to perform a task. Research shows that not all intentions are conscious. Benjamin Libet, a researcher in the fields of physiology and human consciousness and author of *Mind Time*, posits that there is a brief period of time — about one-third of a second — during which anyone can veto even an unconscious intention.

One thing is certain: The more mindful and aware we can become of our intentions, the more free will we possess to cultivate conscious intentions and subsequent actions. An ongoing mindfulness practice can awaken even the subtlest intentions. You might think of these as mind whispers — those intentions that are so gentle and quiet, like a whisper, that they are usually overlooked. Once you start to pay closer attention, you will begin to notice how intentions precede almost everything you do, from generating the smallest movements and everyday behavior to creating a hurricane of violent emotions.

So important is intention in Buddhism that Right Intention — sometimes called Right Thought — is one of the wisdom trainings in the Noble Eightfold Path. Through this training, the mind becomes clear, pure, and directed toward kindness and love. Harsh or harmful thoughts and intentions eventually cease because they can be eliminated almost as soon as they appear on the mind's radar screen. To know whether an intention or thought is harmful or beneficial is vital. Buddha observed: "The thought manifests as the word. The word manifests as the deed. The deed develops into habit. And habit hardens into character. So watch the thought and its way with care, and let it spring from love born out of concern for all beings."[1]

A soft breeze will barely move a leaf on a tree. A tornado will uproot the entire tree. Similarly, everything that happens around you makes its imprint or impression on you, sometimes barely moving the mind while at other times uprooting it. Only by observing the body and the mind can we identify the breeze or tornado that produces our intentions. What impressions are creating those mind whispers? Begin to notice the exact moment when you get a feeling or a sense that you want to indulge in an action or a habit. When it happens, pause and ask yourself, *What thought, intention, or action just preceded this sense or feeling?* If you want to change your life's direction, you need to direct your intention, which means first being honest about the thoughts, rationalizations, intentions, and attitudes you already have.

Even if you can't identify the root cause of a thought, a body sensation, or an intention, you can always introduce another, more beneficial intention in any given moment. The more you pause to notice your feelings and intentions throughout the day, the more awareness of this moment you will enjoy. Over time, you begin to notice thoughts early on, and you can intercept the thoughts you don't want, before they manifest as actions with negative consequences.

One good way to create intentionality is simply to practice it. You can set intentions throughout the day, for breathing, walking, sitting, standing, driving, or talking. Especially catch those moments when your mind creates limiting intentions, with statements such as *I can never do well in school, I'm not very creative,* and *No one really wants to hear what I have to say.* When you catch a negative seed being planted in your mind, let yourself look at it with a sense of neutrality and curiosity. There's no sense in letting negative thoughts create more judgment and blame. Negative thoughts, negative reactivity, and negative intentions regarding others are also limiting and harmful. It is helpful to practice thinking about the happiness and well-being of others, which is also a useful way of turning the mind away from unhealthy intentions. One can also imagine oneself as a fully enlightened being and ask, *What would my enlightened self do?* Another strategy is to set this intention each morning: *I vow to use all skillful means possible to awaken today.* The following practice is designed to cultivate a peaceful field of intention.

Practice intentionality for five minutes at a time in this way: For the next five minutes, set intentions for everything you do. It's easiest to do this in silence and when you will not be interrupted. You can do this with any activity, such as preparing food, eating, driving the car, gardening, or cleaning up the house.

Notice those times when your intention does not originate from the heart or when it is not beneficial for others. Do not blame yourself; instead, allow yourself to begin anew with a genuine effort to open your heart. Keep trying to notice the slivers of craving or desire that creep in, and accept that you are doing the best you can to bring conscious purpose into your daily life. Eventually, you may want to spend up to an entire day practicing mindful intention.

Notes

Epigraph. Sharon Salzberg, "The Power of Intention," DharmaWeb.org, www.dharmaweb.org/index.php/The_Power_of_Intention_by_Sharon _Salzberg (accessed June 2009).

1. Sharon Salzberg, *Loving-Kindness: The Revolutionary Art of Forgiveness* (Boston: Shambhala, 1997), p. 83.

10. Open to Your True Nature

We need, above all else, to nourish our true self — what you could call our Buddha nature — for so often we make the fatal mistake of identifying with our confusion and then use it to judge and condemn ourselves and feed that lack of self-love so many of us suffer from today.

— SOGYAL RINPOCHE

*T*HERE WAS ONCE A BABY EAGLE that fell out of her nest and wandered into a barnyard populated by chickens. The chickens accepted the lost and orphaned baby eagle as one of their own. Since the little eagle grew up among the chickens, she came to believe she was a chicken as well. She did her very best to cluck like a chicken, eat grain like a chicken, and strut like a chicken. Despite embracing her inner chicken-nature, she grew up into a beautiful young eagle, and because the chickens didn't fly, the eagle never stretched out her long wings to discover flight. Then one day all the chickens ran for cover as a large eagle flew overhead. The young eagle ran too. From her hiding place beneath a tree, she peered up at the majestic eagle that glided effortlessly and wished she could soar high in the clouds like an eagle. Alas, the young eagle would never do that as long as she made the mistake of believing she was a chicken.

The truth is that we are all eagles with the capability to soar. This is not about puffing up the ego or the small self and its desires; it is about finding our true nature in order to reach the heights of which we are capable and to free ourselves from the jail of limiting and harmful beliefs.

"I can't finish anything I start," intones Timothy, a handsome twenty-year-old. Though he sounds utterly convincing, my interview with him reveals that he is anything but a slacker or a quitter. I learn that Timothy played football throughout high school and that he currently plays the piano and earns good grades in college. Timothy quietly shares that his girlfriend of one year has broken up with him, leaving him despondent and unmotivated. "I just can't keep a relationship going for very long," he says with his head down and eyes staring at the floor.

"Didn't you say you were a junior in college?" I inquire.

"Yes."

"I thought you said you couldn't finish anything. How'd you finish your first two years of school? How did you get to be a junior?"

"Yeah, that's true. I forgot about that," answers Timothy, with a short laugh.

"And what about the one-year relationship? You didn't quit after one month, or two, or even six months, did you?"

"No, I guess I didn't," he replies, perking up more.

It is obvious that Timothy has a very persuasive but fictional story playing in his head about not being a finisher. There is also the factual story about his life in which he completes what he starts — a story he ignores. At the end of our first session, I give him a simple assignment: make an honest inventory of your strengths. Over time, Timothy learns to recognize and to tell a more accurate and less biased story of his life.

"My mother always told me I was fat, and she put me on diet pills when I was eight years old, even though my weight was normal. Nothing I ever did was good enough," recounts fifty-year-old Anne. While sharing her story, Anne tears up as if the past were happening to her right now, more than forty years after the fact. Throughout our initial session, Anne returns repeatedly to the story of her abuse, her mother's disapproval, and her attempted suicide because of it all. As recently as two months ago, she tells me, she was hospitalized for trying again.

Finally, I say, "Anne, I notice that even when we're talking about something else, you often return to stories about your mother. Have you ever noticed that in daily life?" Anne is silent for a long moment. "Once I tried to count the number of times that I thought about her in a day, but I lost track. I do know that when I'm not thinking about the past or the future, I do a lot better."

For Anne, magnifying the story of her abuse has tinted her entire worldview, like a pair of giant sunglasses. She sees everything through the darkened filter of this narrow story. In the Dhammapada, the Buddha comments on the danger of focusing on a negative narrative, even if it may be true: "'Look how he abused me and beat me, how he threw me down and robbed me.' Live with such thoughts and you live in hate. . . . Abandon such thoughts, and live in love."[1] Because Anne expresses a strong interest in mindfulness, I decide to put up a trial balloon at the conclusion of our session: "One of the things we can work on is creating a healthy detachment from the story you have with your mother. How do you feel about that?"

"I'd like to do that," she says, nodding. But later that week, Anne leaves me a message saying she has enough support at present and doesn't need to return to therapy right now. I am left wondering if she was frightened about letting go of her story of abuse. Sometimes a familiar story, even if it's a painful one, can appear more comforting than the uncertainty, responsibility, and sense of ownership that come with creating a new story.

"My husband's divorce lawyer says I have a depressed personality, and for that reason, I shouldn't get custody of my children," says Margaret while choking back tears. "I guess he's right, since I've been on antidepressant medication for almost a decade." At forty years of age, Margaret is losing everything. Her luxury SUV has been taken away by the finance company. She has lost two houses to foreclosure, her job, all her money and credit through bankruptcy, and, perhaps most distressing, she has temporarily lost custody of her four children. Margaret's entire life and identity as she has known it have been literally repossessed.

Over the year that I work with Margaret, the ground endlessly shifts beneath her. It becomes obvious to her that her sense of identity has been determined entirely by her lifestyle choices. She lived in the fast lane, accumulating more and more stuff until the weight and responsibility of these things became overwhelming and unsustainable. The lifestyle of accumulation became more of a priority than spending quality time with her spouse, and her work schedule led to burnout, constant physical pain, and resentment. Although Margaret seemed to have it all, she felt empty and depressed. Midway in her twenty-year marriage, she began taking antidepressant and anxiety medications. Along the way, she had forgotten who she was, what really mattered to her, and how to find true joy.

I'll never forget my last session with Margaret, which occurred on a monumental day, the day after her divorce papers were finalized in court. She enters the office with a bright countenance — her "sparkle" as she has come to call it. One chapter of her life has been written, and she is eager to begin writing a new chapter. When we discuss what she has learned during this difficult time of transition, Margaret says, "I am now being more true to myself than ever before. I discovered that I'm not a depressed personality like my husband's lawyer said. But I was making choices that drained away my spirit. The next time I get depressed, I'm going to look at the choices I'm making in my life."

The human brain is prewired for narration. The language center in the brains of three-month-old babies lights up when any variety of languages is spoken. Storytelling is perhaps one of the oldest and most profound aspects of being human. Language and stories can give meaning to our lives, and stories can literally shape our reality. As we saw, whether it is a story we tell ourselves (as Timothy did), a story another provides (Anne's mother), a cultural story about what constitutes success (Margaret's life-style choices), or a story about needing to be right or safe at all costs, we need to see how our belief in a story can separate us from our true nature.

Deep down, don't all beings essentially want to be safe, secure, and loved? This is the basic goodness of life. To connect with life in this way is to locate our birthplace and to touch our true nature. When we do this naturally — without being subverted by fear, greed, or craving — we are akin to the plant that knowingly turns its leaves toward the sunlight without effort. But many times abuse can leave us lost in the shadows, unable to find the sun. Filled with fear and anxiety, we may believe that the only way to get what we want is through aggression and violence. War is one way to get safety and demand respect, but it comes at a great cost. Our personal stories can also be driven by greed and craving. We may believe that the only way to attain love and appreciation is through the acquisition of power, control, and external things. But safety doesn't come from being contracted, fearful, and barricaded in a fortress filled with weapons. Love and appreciation cannot grow when we are self-absorbed and grasp at persons, objects, and trophies for our own use.

Have you ever wondered what your life would be like if you could jettison all those years of emotional baggage, confusion, doubt, and ignorance? Our true nature does not need to add something to itself or eliminate something from itself to be what it is. It is present whenever you feel your spirit soar like an eagle. Gandhi called this soul force, or *satyagraha*.

The exercise that follows will support your growing awareness of your unchanging true nature, which is not dependent on the stories of I, me, my, and mine.

Don't let your existing stories frustrate you. Although they are causing you pain, they are also your treasure, for they possess the seeds leading to emergence of the spaciousness of the true self. Find a safe place to sit in silence, perhaps in nature. Identify one of your limiting stories. It could be a story of greed, of needing to win, of trying to control a situation. Sit with the story for several minutes, and breathe deeply as you do this.

Now let yourself contemplate the deep need that lies behind this story — perhaps at its core, this story is about getting love, being needed, feeling safe, or avoiding the pain of shame or loss. Connect with the deeper need this story expresses. Look deeply into the truth of whatever emotions exist in your story or belief — jealousy, envy, lust, fear, hatred, shame, sadness, anger. Don't push these away, but also don't grab onto them. Let them be, and see them for what they are.

Breathe into each emotion that is present, watching each with a gentle understanding. Let spaciousness and emptiness expand around each. As you do this, pay attention to the kernel of nonjealousy, nonenvy, nonlust, nonfear, nonhatred, nonshame, or nonanger that lies dormant. Let it emerge naturally, without expectation, and as you do, just sit with this as it is.

Seeing it as it is. Being it as it is. How *one-derful*!

Notes

Epigraph. Sogyal Rinpoche, *The Spirit of Buddhism: The Future of Dharma in the West* (New York: HarperOne, 2003), p. 65.

1. Thomas Byrom, *Dhammapada: The Sayings of the Buddha* (Boston: Shambhala, 1993), p. 2.

11. Mind Your Mind

The only willful choice one has is the quality of attention
one gives to a thought at any moment.

— JEFFREY SCHWARTZ AND SHARON BEGLEY

*T*HERE WILL BE TIMES when you perceive mindfulness not to be working. At these times, your mind will have a mind of its own, so to speak. You may get frustrated by the mind's stubbornness and astonishing talent for amnesia, as it not only forgets to pay attention but forgets to care about paying attention. It will seem your mind is laughing and sneering at your feckless attempts to train it.

At times like this, you need to be deliberate about seeing clearly. Clear comprehension penetrates the fog so you can more easily see what you see and notice what you notice. It clears up confusion and poor inner-sight in response to questions such as *What is really here in the mind, in consciousness? How can I keep from bumping into the same obstacles over and over? How can I apply more effort and energy toward making mindfulness a priority each day? How can I seek out others who are actively pursuing mindfulness as a life choice?*

It is early in the morning when I visit with Brett for the first time. Within moments of sitting down, the tall twenty-three-year-old with sandy brown hair and a brawny build starts to cry. His story of depression and anxiety began, he tells me, almost nine months earlier when he got his first job, working in retail sales, after graduating college. "My boss complains that I don't try hard enough to sell. But I don't want to push people," he says, his eyes reddening. "Sometimes I get so upset at work that I can hardly go back to the office after lunch. I really wanted to teach music, but I thought I'd see what I could do in the job market. I'd like to quit and go back to school, but if I quit before a year, it won't look good on my résumé."

Brett's job stress and jumbled emotions have thrown him totally off balance. He is unable to clearly see that his job is placing him at odds with his value system and a deeper desire to teach. My work with Brett centers on helping him move toward what really matters most to him. Brett's situation illustrates that clear comprehension is difficult to attain when we feel scattered, dismiss our inner wisdom, deplete or exhaust ourselves, or struggle with confidence. Any of these may be a sign that your life is out of balance, making it difficult for you to observe the mind with discipline and clarity.

When this occurs, ask yourself the following two questions. First, *Am I conducting myself in a way that is harmful either to myself or to others?* If you identify harmful actions, it's important to change course as soon as you can. The second question to ask yourself is, *Am I behaving inappropriately?* Another version of this would be, *Are my intentions misguided in some way?* For example, you may be working hard at a job, which could be beneficial, but your intention to do so may be driven by greed, lust, or another inappropriate emotion. When you answer these questions honestly, you establish the ability within yourself to remove the confusion that makes it hard to mind the mind.

When we mind the mind, we don't need to throw anything out. There's nothing to change or to do. By honestly and directly facing a situation, you begin to remove the obstacles of confusion that make it hard to focus on the mind. Regardless of what is present in the mind, you can observe its contents: anger, joy, boredom, depression, frustration, bare awareness, judgmental thoughts, nonjudgmental thoughts, cravings, avoidance, grasping, attachments, liberation, nonliberation.

Let all into the room, friends and enemies alike. Let them mingle and see what happens. Let all drops of thought rise from the depths and merge back into the ocean of consciousness from whence they came. Remember, too, that minding the mind means going beyond the analytical mind to apprehend and penetrate the impermanent nature of mental phenomena. Observing and investigating the mind lead to insight and freedom. We enlighten the mind by letting it be just as it is.

Congratulations on completing the mind key teachings. They offer profound ways for us to touch the moment with awareness and bare observation. You have peered behind the veil to observe the most elemental instrument of consciousness, your own mind. As you continue to observe and enhance your life with these trainings, may you bring an attitude of curiosity and acceptance to each awakened moment.

We wrap up the mind key with an overall approach for applying these teachings.

Review all the mind key teachings to find one that resonates with you right now. Make a commitment to practice this particular teaching each day for the next week. If the teaching you choose involves daily practice for a regular period of time, set an amount of time you want to practice each day.

Begin with a goal that is small, realistic, and achievable. So if that means five minutes a day, that's great. You can always add an extra five minutes when you want. Basically, it's important to build up your confidence and effort. After a week of practice, you may want to move on to another mind key teaching, but don't feel compelled to switch if you're getting a lot out of the practice you are currently using. You can always add a second practice to the first and see how that works for you.

Note

Epigraph. Jeffrey Schwartz and Sharon Begley, *The Mind and the Brain: Neuroplasticity and the Power of Mental Force* (New York: ReganBooks, 2002), p. 310.

PART TWO

THE BODY KEY

*T*HE BODY IS PERHAPS THE MOST IDEAL VEHICLE for experiencing the here and now. Each of the teachings in the body key reveals the code with which you can enter the present moment. Be patient as the body's code is revealed to you, and enjoy the process of learning how the body is both a teacher and a student.

12. Breathe Consciously and Mindfully

Learn to be calm and you will always be happy.

— PARAMHANSA YOGANANDA

FOR CENTURIES, OUR WISDOM TRADITIONS have told of a sacred connection between the breath and the divine. Archaeologists have found statues in India dating to 2000 BCE that depict people in yogic positions associated with breathing. The ancient Sanskrit word *prana* refers to the essence of the life force itself. In Buddhism, the breath is a microcosm through which one can gain insight into all phenomena; it is a way to directly comprehend the nature of impermanence, grasping, and letting go. The Hebrew word *ruach* is often translated as "the divine spirit" in the Old Testament and literally means "breath." The Bible says that God breathed life into Adam, and in receiving God's breath, Adam was filled with the essence of God. Even today, Native Americans such as the Zuni continue to express spirit with words that also denote the wind and the breath. Can the simple act of breathing help us to recover this link to our deepest self?

It is a hectic day at the hospital clinic where I am working. After opening the door to a filled waiting room, I call out the name Bernard and am greeted by a pale, gangly man in his late thirties, who springs up from his seat as if he is on fire. Moments later, sitting in my office, he wrings his hands and looks to be in a great deal of pain. When I ask what brings him into the clinic, Bernard tells me that he suffers from anxiety and panic attacks, even in the classroom where he teaches as a college professor. That's not all. Fear and anxiety haunt several areas of his life. He finds it harder and harder to leave his apartment and fears flying in airplanes. When he discloses that in staff meetings he finds it nearly impossible to speak, I notice that his right hand moves up to grip his throat as if he is choking.

"I've had these problems my whole life," he tells me with a tone of defeat, adding that his mother and father were very anxious as well. In particular, Bernard is worried about an upcoming trip to visit his elderly mother in another state. Bernard is not sure he can make the flight without going into a full-blown panic attack. Together, we work on a treatment plan that utilizes several strategies to help him cope with his anxiety and panic. But the core skill he learns is diaphragmatic breathing.

After a week of practice, Bernard returns to my office and sits down with a grin on his face. "You're smiling," I comment. "Did something good happen that you can tell me about?" Excitedly, Bernard shares the story of how he felt a panic attack coming on while teaching a class. Then he remembered the diaphragmatic breathing posture I taught him. The feeling of panic subsided, and the students never knew that their professor was entering a state of deep relaxation right in front of them.

How many breaths do you take in a day? Close your eyes and count your breaths for the next minute. If you do the math, you will discover that we take approximately twenty thousand breaths a day. And yet, how many of those breaths are we consciously aware of? This is exactly how we unlock mindfulness — by taking what is unconscious and shining the light of consciousness on it. By intentionally taking a diaphragmatic breath (aka belly breath), we turn on the body's innate relaxation system and thermostat.

What is more, to notice the breath is to appreciate our own precious being and to contact the essence of our presence. With the breath, we peer behind the veil at how we come into this world needing and gasping for the breath of life. Holding onto the breath leads to suffocation. Living requires a constant letting go. This in itself is a powerful lesson in nonattachment. Each breath teaches us that holding on too long to anything creates pain and suffering. Letting go is nature's way, and this is no small thing.

From the physical perspective, it only takes three conscious diaphragmatic breaths to reduce our blood pressure, pulse rate, and respiration rate; to cleanse the blood of lactate; and to generate alpha brain waves, which put us in "the zone."

Diaphragmatic breathing also releases serotonin, the mood-stabilizing neurotransmitter, into our bloodstream. Perhaps most astonishing of all is that belly breathing can accomplish this in only twenty seconds.

Physiologically, breathing into the deepest part of our lungs pushes on the diaphragmatic wall, the muscle that separates the chest and abdominal cavities. The downward movement of the diaphragm compresses the abdomen and forces it outward. This in turn causes the gut to press on the vagus nerve (a bundle of cranial nerves running down the inside of the spine), which triggers the relaxation response and releases serotonin from the gut into the bloodstream to take to the brain.

When we breathe shallowly, or high in the chest, we don't get these benefits. In fact, chest breathing makes us vulnerable to the body's alert-and-alarm system, the fight-or-flight syndrome that floods the body and brain with the stress hormones adrenaline and cortisol. After just three to four days of this, your body enters a chronic stress state, which Bernard's story shows us is debilitating. It adversely affects our sleep, creates cravings for high-fat foods and sugar, and inhibits our immune system, even destroying T cells and NK (natural killer) cells, which the body uses to defend itself from sickness. Breathing mindfully and consciously to de-stress the body is a form of self-healing. It's also worth mentioning that conscious breathing trumps the stress response because both of these systems cannot operate at the same time. The brain-body wants to cool itself down from stress, and it could use assistance.

Now, let's try this for real. Forget anything you may have previously heard about counting and holding your breath, and don't worry about whether to breathe through your nose or

mouth. Just do what comes naturally, as long as you are getting air into the deeper part of your lungs. To begin, observe
whether you are breathing into your chest or your belly. You
can do this by placing the palm of one hand directly on your
chest and the other on your belly as you breathe normally. If the
hand over your chest is moving or both hands are moving, you
are taking shallow breaths. Only when your lower hand is moving are you breathing fully into the belly. (If you feel light-
headed or dizzy, then you may be taking too deep of a breath.)
Taking a breath is like pouring water into a glass: the bottom
fills up first, and if you keep pouring, the upper half gets full.
The point of conscious breathing is to move air to the lower
lungs with a normal breath. And if you are still not sure which
hand is moving, look in the mirror as you breathe.

If you are a chest breather, don't worry. We are all born to
breathe diaphragmatically. Look at any baby and you will notice its little belly rising and falling with each breath. We are
designed to belly breathe. Our ribs are interlaced with muscles
called the intercostals; the intercostals hinge the ribs open so
we can take a deeper breath. With conscious breathing, we are
relearning to breathe the way nature intends. Stretching the intercostals is easy to do. Clasp your hands behind your back. (If
you are sitting in a chair, you may want to scoot forward to do
this.) Notice that this is the same arm position soldiers use when
they assume the "at ease" stance. Observe your breath. Do you
notice your abdomen rising or expanding more now that you
are opening your rib cage? (If you are a woman who feels uncomfortable about your stomach moving outward because of
cultural conditioning around the shape of women's bellies,
practice in private.) Are your stomach muscles relaxed? They

need to be for diaphragmatic breathing, so soften the abdominal muscles whenever you practice.

Another position that opens the rib cage and makes belly breathing easier has us place our hands behind our head, elbows out to the side. This is the same posture athletes often take to get a deeper breath after exerting themselves. Again, observe where the air is going with each breath. Which position — hands behind the back or hands behind the head — works best for you? You can also belly breathe effectively while standing up.

It is important to integrate conscious breathing into our lifestyle. You may experience a sense of calm after breathing like this. You may even want to laugh. Let your body experience whatever feeling occurs. Belly breathing can be done when lying on the back or side, which means you can always practice at night in bed. With enough practice, belly breathing can become your default method of breathing.

Try the following practice to boost the amount of time you spend cooling down your brain and body from stress.

This is a good way to jump-start the practice of using diaphragmatic breath. Get some colored stickers and place them in different locations as reminders to consciously belly breathe for one minute. Place one on your alarm clock to remind you to breathe diaphragmatically first thing in the morning. You can stick them on the bathroom mirror, the refrigerator, and so on. At work, consider placing stickers on your computer or appointment book. Attach another to the rearview mirror in your car. With practice, you will invite the joy of conscious breathing into all parts of your day, and over time, you will start to notice whether your breath is shallow or deep. By bringing breath into your field of awareness, you will retrain your body to use its natural thermostat to manage stress.

Note

Epigraph. Diane Durston, *Wabi Sabi: The Art of Everyday Life* (North Adams, MA: Storey Publishing, 2006), p. 301.

13. Slow Down and Enjoy the View

Life is not hurrying on to a receding future,
nor hankering after the imagined past. It is the turning aside
like Moses to the miracle of the lit bush.

— R. S. THOMAS

*I*T IS THROUGH AN ATTITUDE OF WILLINGNESS and openness that the mind and heart broaden their capacity for fulfillment and joy. Slowing down and being present does not
mean things will be the way we want or expect them to be.
What's asked for, instead, is to witness the wonder of things as
they are. By doing so, we build a bridge to a spaciousness that
shifts narrow-mindedness and judgment, and emotional stingi-
ness and constriction. This spaciousness is sturdy enough and
big enough to contain whatever is present, joy or suffering.
When we slow our body down to the pace of nature, we touch
and are touched by the world in a tender and special way.

It is early afternoon, and I have just finished lunch with a friend in an older neighborhood of Portland, Oregon, known as Sellwood. I feel the impulse to hurry back home — after all, there's always work to do, always another item on the schedule. But while walking back to the car, I notice a name stamped into the concrete sidewalk. This is not the scribbling of a child, but a legibly written name and date. Now I notice other inscribed names that go back to the turn of the previous century, from 1912 through 1916. It would be all too easy to ignore these unusual markings and get back on the fast track, obsessed with what is off in the future, the "yet undone" as I call it. Instead, I take a conscious breath to slow down and allow myself to settle into this place, this setting, this present moment. I decide to leave the fast track to follow the trail of names and cracks that tell the story of this old sidewalk.

I cannot help but marvel at this historical remnant. Most often, our cities wash away the past to make room for the newer, the bigger, and the better — a creed most often accepted without question. But here, a foot-trodden link to the past connects one to a time and a place where neighbors sat on front porches, chatting and sipping iced tea under the oaks. I crane my head and look up at a nearby home. The highly canted roof and delicately scalloped wooden trim are testament to an age when people learned a trade and cared enough to inscribe names, such as Johnson and O'Neill, in concrete. *I was here. I mattered*, they seem to say.

In search of similar markings, my friend joins me, and we wander off the curbs and onto the streets, meandering like stray cats. Even though traffic is minimal, I find it extremely difficult to be mindful of cars when my nose is pointed toward the ground. Although some of the original concrete street remains, we do not find inscriptions there like those found on the sidewalk. I do notice, however, several ornate manhole covers engraved with images of roses. Portland's moniker is Rose City. I wonder about a connection. I also observe that street names, some of which are now obsolete, are stamped on the corners of the curbs.

Some thirty minutes later, we notice that we have traveled several blocks from where our car is parked. Heading back, I observe the leafy oaks, a tall cypress, and other trees, likely planted when these homes were originally built. Not only have I followed my curiosity in a way that gives me a little insight into my adopted city, but also the act of slowing down has helped me create an enduring memory. I have fully accepted this positive experience into my being.

We have all experienced how even one-time negative or traumatic events can stay with us for the rest of our lives. This is a survival adaptation that helps to protect us (as it did our ancestors) by permanently imprinting potential danger on our memory. Instead of facing our ancestors' life-threatening predators, today we confront other stress-inducing events that trigger the body's same ancient fight-or-flight response in a matter of seconds. This is why traumatic events can create powerful memories and flashbacks, which can continue for years.

However, it takes a good twenty to thirty minutes to form an equally enduring positive memory. Consider life a rainbow that offers many colors, and for whatever darkness exists in life, we owe it to ourselves to absorb the full range of colors into our experience and memory. Even apparently normal moments are easy to gloss over unless, like Moses, we slow down and turn toward the miracle that is before us, however small, ordinary, and seemingly insignificant. Try the exercise below to consciously engage in a slower pace of life and to enjoy the brightness and richness this pace invites.

Make a conscious effort to slow down for fifteen to twenty minutes at least once a day, even if you need to schedule this time into your day planner. Use the time to cultivate a positive and enduring memory. This might mean taking a mindful walk, giving your body a rest, meditating, seeking out nature's beauty, savoring food, or enjoying a new locale. Use slow-down time to steep yourself in whatever experience you are having — washing the dishes, clearing the clutter, taking a shower. Engage in whatever experience you are having with a sense of ease and full awareness.

Note

Epigraph. Robert Atwan, George Dardess, and Peggy Rosenthal, eds., *Divine Inspiration: The Life of Jesus in World Poetry* (New York: Oxford University Press, 1997), p. 229.

14. Experience Full Presence of Body

He lived at a little distance from his body,
regarding his own acts with doubtful side-glances.

— JAMES JOYCE

$\mathcal{A}$ WEEK AFTER I HAD DEMONSTRATED body awareness to
a meditation group, a member returned with a big gauze
bandage covering her thumb. Maybe I could have been more
mindful of my speech, but the bandage was so hard to miss that
I couldn't help asking her what happened. She held her band-
aged thumb high in the air for the entire meditation class to see
and then declared, without any hint of blame or shame, "I was
making a salad, and I got distracted and lost mindfulness of my
body." She stated what happened without adornment — what
a skillful mindfulness student.

In the animated film *WALL·E*, the humans of the future live
on a massive spaceship with hi-tech machines that provide for
all their needs. Because the humans are obese (whether from
lack of movement, too much food, or both is hard to say), they
never walk, moving about instead in levitating reclining chairs

that resemble Barcaloungers on steroids. At one point in the story, human survival depends on the ability of one man, the ship's captain, to literally stand up and take a few steps.

When we lose our connection to the body, we lose one of our most important capacities for mindfulness. Right now, raise both of your arms out to the side. Close your eyes, and bring your arms slowly together until your palms touch. How were you able to know where your body was in space with your eyes closed? We possess a natural sense known as proprioception, which is the ability to inwardly perceive the body's spatial orientation in movement, moment by moment. Although you may largely live in your head, you can always return home to the body, the vital sense of being with which you took your first breath.

A high-powered and successful attorney in his mid-fifties, James greets me in the waiting room with an upright stance and a head of thick black hair that together make him seem taller than he is. Immaculately dressed in a suit and tie, he shakes my hand with an overly strong grip. His dark brown eyes are intense. James gives the impression of a successful general ready to command an army.

Moments later, in my office, James's posture transforms when I ask him what brings him to see me. His shoulders slump, his eyes dim, and his hands fold clumsily in his lap. "I feel inadequate. I have felt this way since my teens, and it's affecting my work and my relationships to a point where I . . . I just don't have much hope," he says, his voice trailing off. Now I no longer see the confident head of his own law firm sitting before me, but a sad, little boy plagued by negative and self-critical thoughts.

Over time, James shares stories that capture how he "never measured up" for his angry and demanding alcoholic father. James married three times, and each time found shortcomings in his partner that he could not abide. Although he badly wants a loving relationship, James is always finding fault, his mind critical of both the person he tries to get to know and himself. When James converses with women, his mind chatters loudly internally in a self-demeaning commentary: *You said the wrong thing again! Can't you see that she's too beautiful for someone like you? No matter how much you try, she will eventually discover that you are not good enough.*

During our work together, James starts to recognize that his blaming mind is not factual but is playing an old script, which is opinionated, distorted, and judgmental. He begins to realize that his critical mind almost instantly puts things into polarizing categories: black and white, good and bad, success and failure, right and wrong. Though we make progress in helping James to create a new inner script, he is very good at defending his critical mind — as any successful lawyer should be.

Fortunately, the path of the body bypasses that of the mind. Slowly we work on getting James into his body. Then one day, I ask if he is willing to see what it would be like to inhabit his body moment to moment. I tell him that we can do this together and that I will lead. He agrees. I start by grounding James in his body, having him mindfully sense his feet on the ground, his legs on the chair, and so forth. After a few minutes of guided imagery and breathing, I tell James that we will now share our moment-to-moment experiences in the body. "I feel a slight tension in my shoulders," I tell him. "There is a lightness in my face, a feeling of calm. The area around my mouth almost feels like it is ready to smile and laugh." I share for three or four minutes, tuning into and describing my sense being, which is the essence of the body's feeling state — whether an overall feeling of comfort and ease, fear, anxiety, uncertainty, anger, dread, lightness, tightness, and so on. I describe my sense being as "light and at ease, like a balloon that is neither underfilled nor overfilled," and then I ask James to start.

He speaks haltingly at first, "I feel a stiffness in my neck," and then faster, "I'm feeling this is stupid and silly."

"Does your body feel this is stupid and silly, or is your mind saying this is stupid and silly?" I ask softly.

"My mind says it."

"Stay with what the body is experiencing," I coach him.

James continues, looking and sounding uneasy. Although his mind frequently interrupts, he becomes increasingly aware that it is his mind, not his body, that is commenting negatively. After about five minutes, something happens. The pained expression on James's face slowly dissolves, and as he gets into his body, his mind grows quiet.

"There's this tightness around my chest," he reports with a quizzical expression.

"Tell me more."

"It's always there, a heaviness, like it's guarded, like there's a wall."

"This is your sense being. See if you can locate it more closely."

There is a long pause before James responds, "My heart. It's around my heart."

"Imagine you can breathe joy and happiness into that part of your body now," I instruct him. "Breathe warmth and compassion into your heart. See if you can create some space for yourself away from that wall and its heaviness. As you do this, notice if you feel less guarded, more tender and open."

James takes slow, deliberate breaths. His body seems to relax more, and his chest heaves. Tears well up in his eyes. "Yes, I can feel this part of my body opening. There is less heaviness around the chest."

"How does that feel for you?" I ask.

"It feels good, like there's a sense of wholeness. It's a feeling I haven't known before."

When we conclude the exercise, James is surprised to find that fifteen minutes have passed. He is excited to discover that being guarded around his chest can be felt and experienced and that it does not have to be feared and avoided. Most importantly, James learned that he could sit with it and soften it. These are important skills to have for locating and healing areas of trauma and old pain. As James processes his experience, we talk about how he can continue to get into his body, even when he is at his job. This is challenging work, I concede, but it can be done. When James leaves the office, he seems to beam, like a child who has discovered something very precious, which he has.

The body excels at locating the present moment — there is no way, of course, to take a breath for yesterday or tomorrow. The body also helps us identify what old burdens of pain we are carrying around with us. These are its blessings. So, if you find that your mind is too critical, that you easily become anxious, or that you often worry about the future, you stand to benefit from the following strategy, which centers your attention in present time by using the body.

When you find yourself getting anxious, worried, or lost in your thoughts, gently return to the body by pressing your palms together softly. As you do this, notice how far up your arm the tension goes (to your wrists, elbows, shoulders, etc.). Now press your palms together even harder. Do you feel heat building in your hands? You can also dig your heels into the ground and notice what sensations are present in them. You can also notice the sensations on your fingertips as they type on the keyboard when you are working on the computer. Feel the sensation of warmth or coolness from your mouse. Observe your posture. Practice bringing attention to the body in your other daily circumstances as well. Whenever you lose contact with the body, connect again simply by noticing sensations as they come and go with a sense of neutrality and openness.

Note

Epigraph. James Joyce, *Dubliners* (New York: Oxford University Press, 2008), p. 83.

15. Find Balance and Detoxify Stress

It's wonderful that we are so adaptable, but there are some things we should not adapt to. . . . Our brains and nervous systems were designed by nature to be part of nature. To live in an artificial world makes us exotic, fragile, easily damaged.

— RICHARD O'CONNOR

AN AMERICAN MECHANICAL ENGINEER by the name of Frederick Taylor published a monograph in 1911 titled "The Principles of Scientific Management" that forever changed the way we perceive our relationship to work. Taylor believed that workers would be more efficient if they did not think and their behavior were strictly tied to the clock. Although this new paradigm of bringing the clock and efficiency into the workplace was resisted at first — even investigated by Congress for being anti-worker — this viewpoint not only took hold but also has become our gold standard.

The emphasis on productivity at all costs has made us view ourselves mechanically. We push ourselves to new limits, taking work home, avoiding vacations, and transforming lunch — once a bastion of social connection and relaxation — into an efficient and joyless activity meant to refuel our physical engines. We have become obedient machines, living to work instead of working to live. But we are not machines. And we are not immune to the effects of perpetual stress or even perceived stress.

One of the most revealing studies about stress comes from psychologist Elissa Epel and Nobel Prize–winning cellular biologist Elizabeth Blackburn. In a 2004 study, they investigated how stress affects us at the cellular level to accelerate aging.[1] They studied a highly stressed-out group, mothers of chronically ill children. After the women were put through a series of stress-inducing tests, telomeres in the chromosomes of their immune cells were examined. Telomeres, which are located at the ends of the chromosomes, help to hold the cells together. We age because of the natural thinning and shortening of telomeres that occur over time. When the telomere is no longer able to protect the cell, that cell dies.

Epel and Blackburn found that it was not just stress but also perceived stress that shortened telomeres in the mothers. In a *60 Minutes II* interview about their study, Blackburn says, "The shorter the telomeres were, the worse stress people had had. . . . It was as though there had been in excess of ten years of extra aging in these individuals' blood cells. . . . And that's actually an underestimate."[2] Epel makes an important psychological observation when she says, "The cell is not a closed system. . . . What happens in the mind, in particular, perceptions of stress, can indeed affect the most fundamental unit of our physical beings."[3] Epel and Blackburn also discovered that the women who maintained a positive attitude and distanced themselves from stressful events had healthy telomeres.

In the bigger picture, we can think of stress as our body's expression of its daily experiences. In 2006, Emma K. Adam, a psychologist and professor at Northwestern University, published her study's finding that cortisol levels react to our daily experiences.[4] Those who go to bed feeling lonely wake up with higher levels of cortisol than those who don't go to bed feeling lonely. The study also found that individuals who experience anger and troubles throughout the day build up more cortisol by bedtime. This response may be adaptive in the short term, as Dr. Adam explains: "Cortisol helps us respond to stressful experiences and do something about them. It is necessary for survival — fluctuations in this hormone assist us in meeting the changing demands we face in our daily lives. You've gone to bed with loneliness, sadness, feelings of being overwhelmed, then along comes a boost of hormones in the morning to give you the energy you need to meet the demands of the day. High levels of cortisol in the evening are a kind of biological signature of a bad day."[5]

Fortunately, we can return to a natural state of harmony and detoxify stress chemicals from the body and brain by taking one-minute balance breaks during the day. When I conduct workshops, I make a point of inserting a slide into my normal program that poses the question, *Where are you now?* I explain to the group that whenever this slide comes up, we will stop what we are doing and just be present. We spend a minute in silence, resting in the present moment. We no longer focus on learning, on doing this or that, but just on being in the moment. Let's explore this exercise.

Where are you now? Where was your mind in the moments before you saw these words? Perhaps you were thinking about something you would be doing in the future; perhaps you had a thought about a conversation or interaction from the past. Or maybe you half-remember thinking about something but aren't sure. Do you see how the mind can travel? How one thought leads to another and then another? In this moment, I want you to notice your posture. Sit up; try not to let your body slump. Feel yourself sitting with a sense of dignity and grace. Observe the sensation of your feet on the floor. Take a few seconds to push your heels into the floor and ground your feet to the earth.

Notice your breath. Begin to use the diaphragmatic breathing method we learned earlier. If it helps to move your arms behind you to get a deeper breath, go ahead and make that movement. Notice whether the breaths are of equal length, without trying to make it one way or the other. Just let the rhythm of breathing be natural and effortless. Let each breath rise and fall, like waves in the ocean, coming and going. Let go a little more with each breath. There is nothing to hold on to. How easy it is to let go!

Finally, observe any tension or tightness that may be residing in your body at this time. Many people find tension around the neck and shoulder area. Remember that tension is often cumulative. You may not feel much stress when you wake up in the morning, but it creeps up slowly throughout the day as you encounter stress. Wherever this stress has settled in your body, imagine that your next breath enters through the top of your head and flows easily to that part of your body, filling it up and creating space and ease from the tension. Imagine that a cleansing breath absorbs this tension and that when you exhale it is carried with other impurities down through the body and out through the bottom of your feet.

In this way, the buildup of tension is deposited deep into the earth for composting. Continue to take more purifying breaths, letting each inhalation create spaciousness from stress, pain, tightness, and each exhalation carry the tension out of your feet and into the earth. You may notice tension releasing in the body. Your shoulders or another part of your body may relax a little. Enjoy feeling softer and more relaxed.

As happens with any focused practice, thoughts, sounds, memories, or sensations will temporarily grab your attention. Simply notice, and then gently, kindly, return to the breath and the process of breathing into the tension. If you don't feel any tension (good for you), let the rhythm of breath flow throughout your body with a sense of peace and presence.

Now that you understand the process, try a one-minute balance break on your own. You can time yourself with a wristwatch or clock. Sometimes it's better to close your eyes and just count nine or ten breaths; that way you can really focus on the body and the breath. When you have finished, slowly open your eyes and let yourself return to your surrounding environment.

What did that balance break feel like for you? Frequently,

participants in workshops describe their experiences as calming, relaxing, or refreshing. Some report that after only a couple of balance breaks, they begin to look forward to the next one. In general, most are surprised at how quickly stress appears in the body and at how effectively we can help to dissolve and release it. It's always good to hear people share that although their mind was off in the future when the slide appeared, coming to this awareness in itself helps them become more centered. Occasionally, there is mention of impatience, of not wanting to slow down to be present. I sometimes experience impatience when my presentation gets interrupted. But after a few moments of breathing, that fleeting sense of impatience gives way as I engage in the moment-to-moment process of regaining balance.

Balance breaks are especially good to take during times of uncertainty and transition. Do a balance break while driving, before a meeting, while standing in line, or any time that a stress-inducing event is on the horizon. Here is a beneficial and practical way to implement one-minute balance breaks in your day.

Practice taking a balance break at least once each morning, even if you don't think you need it. Take another during your lunch break and one more later in the afternoon. Remember, we're talking only three minutes here. If you can't take three minutes out of the day to bring balance to yourself, then you need to evaluate your lifestyle and values.

Notes

Epigraph. Richard O'Connor, *Undoing Perpetual Stress: The Missing Connection Between Depression, Anxiety, and 21st Century Illness* (New
  York: Berkley, 2006), p. 53.

1. Elissa Epel, Elizabeth Blackburn, Jue Lin, Firdaus Dhabhar, Nancy
    Adler, Jason Morrow, and Richard Cawthon, "Accelerated Telomere
    Shortening in Response to Life Stress," *Proceedings of the National Acad-
    emy of Sciences of the United States of America* (2004), www.pnas.org/
    content/101/49/17312.full (accessed June 2009).

2. Brian Dakss, "Aging: The Stress Factor," *CBS News*, www.cbsnews.com/
    stories/2005/08/25/60II/main796002_page2.shtml?tag=content
    Main;contentBody (accessed June 2009).

3. Ibid.

4. Emma K. Adam, Louise C. Hawkley, Brigitte M. Kudielka, and
    John T. Cacioppo, "Day-to-Day Dynamics of Experience — Corti-
    sol Associations in a Population-Based Sample of Older Adults," *Pro-
    ceedings of the National Academy of Sciences of the United States of
    America* (2006), www.pnas.org/content/103/45/17058.full (accessed
    June 2009).

5. Pat Vaughan Tremmel, "People Who Go to Bed Lonely Get Stress
    Hormone Boost Next Morning," Institute for Policy Research, North-
    western University, www.northwestern.edu/ipr/news/adam.html
    (accessed June 2009).

16. Make Peace with Food, Eating, and Hunger

I've been on a constant diet for the last two decades.
I've lost a total of 789 pounds.
By all accounts, I should be hanging from a charm bracelet.

—— ERMA BOMBECK

Everything you see I owe to spaghetti.

—— SOPHIA LOREN

WHY DO SO MANY OF US STRUGGLE to find balance with food and eating? We live in an age when food is plentiful in many parts of the world, as well as an age when the complexity of our relationship with food includes psychological disorders ranging from food addictions and obsessive compulsiveness to chronic stress and maladaptive attempts to control childhood trauma. Not only is food a convenient way to medicate difficult feelings, but we are also genetically wired to behave as if food were scarce. Our bodies constantly monitor for hunger. Even when we are well fed, when it comes to food, we behave like squirrels in their seasonal hunt for more food to stow away. Finding peace with food can be hard.

When we accept the truth of our complex relationship with food, we take the first step toward understanding the power of food, and more compassionate ways of relating to food become possible. For example, instead of fighting with food — through diets, overeating, bingeing and purging, and being preoccupied with it all of our waking hours — we can learn to gently invite food into our body and soul as a friend. Food has much to teach us about ourselves — our cravings and desires, our connection to all living things, our responsibilities to the care of the planet, and our capacity for joy. When we become conscious about food, we create a healthier relationship with it.

It is all too easy to forget or to ignore that eating food is a spiritual experience, intimate and unique. Perhaps this is why many wisdom traditions use food as a metaphor for attaining some of the highest ideals. For Buddhists, food represents a path to moderation, or the middle way; for Christians, it offers an opportunity to practice tolerance and charity. In Islam, food signifies moderation and personal responsibility; in Judaism, it symbolizes the greater purpose of honoring life as blessed and holy.

Consider for a moment the nature of food that originates as a plant. All plants are alive and dynamic, as we are. Plants absorb sunlight, water, carbon dioxide, and nutrients from the soil. A tomato plant, banana tree, or other plant may not have the same type of sentience we have, but all plants do produce oxygen to support the respiration of a vast array of organisms. In turn, these organisms, including humans, produce the carbon dioxide that supports plant life.

That we dance in concert with an interconnected web of life, dependent on one another, has long been recognized by many cultures as sacred. Many Native American tribes, for example, harvest only part of any crop. They also emphasize showing appreciation to the animals and plants whose lives we take for nourishment. To this day, many cultures experience food as a community gathering, whether wading into rice paddies while singing in unison or dancing under the stars in preparation for a fruitful harvest.

Here is something to contemplate: Only living food that grows on our planet is suitable for our bodies to transform into the energy and sustenance we need. How could our bodies possibly achieve this miracle if we were not made up of the same basic stuff as such food? Every meal can help us grasp this concept a little more. As life sciences writer Lyall Watson points out in *Gifts of Unknown Things*: "We did not come into this world. We came out of it, like buds out of branches and butterflies out of cocoons. We are a natural product of this earth, and if we turn out to be intelligent beings, then it can only be because we are fruits of an intelligent earth."[1]

This perspective informs a more compassionate understanding of food. When we ingest foods that are unnatural — including artificial ingredients, genetically modified foods with new molecules unknown to the human body, and inert substances and preservatives — we sever our natural connection to the earth and deny its sanctity in the greater scheme. We dishonor nature, including the nature of our own body, mind, and soul. Food does not originate from a grocery or a convenience store. As Carl Sagan said, "If you wish to make an apple pie from scratch, you must first invent the universe."[2]

Becoming more conscious about our relationship to food also involves the act of eating mindfully, skills we can learn and practice. Unlike strict diets, which research shows lead to feelings of failure and low self-esteem when the regimen inevitably can't be maintained, mindful eating focuses on a lifelong skill set. The truth is that our eating habits didn't develop overnight and won't go away overnight. The worst that can happen at any meal is that you may be less mindful, but you can always become more skillfully present with the next bite and the next meal. Such a patient and hopeful perspective cannot fail to help us develop as mindful eaters, establishing a sane and realistic relationship with food.

So, where do you start? If you want to manage your food, first manage your stress. This step alone will help you become more conscious with food. For example, try breathing diaphragmatically for one minute before sitting down to eat or when you are transitioning to a meal. Let yourself become aware of your emotions, because emotions can trigger our less conscious eating habits.

Second, practice slowing down while eating. This will allow you to notice your hunger cues and satiation levels since it takes up to about twenty minutes for the brain's appetite center to get the signal that you have eaten enough. We often overeat before we sense our body's fullness. It's important to get in the habit of eating in synch with the body's hunger instead of eating with our sense of vision alone — for example, finishing all that we have on our plate.

Third, do your best to eat without distraction, at least some of the time. Many people who binge eat or overeat make the mistake of treating food and mealtime as an afterthought. What difference would it make if you were to create an island of peace around your meal? Don't answer the phone, work on the computer, or watch television while eating, and see for yourself how these changes affect your relationship with food.

Become friends with your hunger. If food will not satisfy the feeling you have, then you may not be experiencing physical hunger. Don't be afraid of the sensation of hunger; it does not define who you are. Hunger is a signal your body sends you to let you know that it needs nourishment and energy. Instead of voraciously eating according to the strength of your appetite, ask yourself: How much food and what kind of food will satisfy this hunger? Also, try rating your hunger on a one-to-ten scale before each meal, where one equals no hunger and ten equals extreme hunger. Eating when your hunger falls in the four-to-six range should help you to eat more moderately and avoid overeating because of extreme hunger.

Notes

Epigraphs. Dick Enberg, ed., *Dick Enberg's Humorous Quotes for All Occasions*, with Brian and Wendy Morgan (Kansas City, MO: Andrews McMeel, 2000), p. 96; John Dickie, *Delizia!: The Epic History of the Italians and Their Food* (New York: Free Press, 2008), p. 29.

1. Lyall Watson, *Gifts of Unknown Things* (Rochester, VT: Destiny Books, 1991).

2. Carl Sagan, *Cosmos* (New York: Ballantine Books, 1985), p. 179.

17. Wake Up to a Cosmic Smile

*Your body is your only home in the universe.... The body is such
an intricate and complex place. The more you become aware
of what a nuanced inner network it is, the more you wonder how
it actually continues to function in secrecy and silence.*

— JOHN O'DONOHUE

*I*MET JOHN O'DONOHUE once at a national conference
where we both spoke. I am grateful to have been touched
by his special wit, grace, and lightness of being. John spent
many years as a priest in Ireland before leaving the priesthood
to follow the call of philosophy and spirituality as a writer and
speaker. When I joined John at a table near the back of a large
room during a presentation, we shared some thoughts, but
mostly laughs. He was extraordinarily gifted at finding the levity in life, and his lightness seemed to spread through his entire
being, from the lilting Irish brogue in his voice to the broad
smile and flicker of amusement in his eyes. During this brief
meeting, I was touched by the openness and grace he shared —
not just his thoughts but also his hearty handshake and the way
his entire body seemed to move in concert with every moment's

fresh awakening. He was fully integrated; his body appeared connected in a way that left absolutely nothing behind.

The Cosmic Smile, or Healing Universal Smile as it is sometimes called, is an ancient practice used in Buddhism and some other traditions. It is a direct way to acknowledge our body, its wisdom, and its connection to mind and spirit. The Cosmic Smile is not a relaxation exercise, however; it is actually a proactive way to scan the motor sensory cortex of the brain. If at any time you feel uncomfortable — because of a body memory, trauma, or injury — please stop and open your eyes. Allow yourself to create space away from the discomfort. If an overwhelming negative feeling persists, you may want to seek professional help.

To begin, assume a comfortable position, whether sitting in a chair or lying down on a mat. Some people prefer lying down with their feet and lower legs resting on a chair. Once you are situated, take a few centering breaths. Notice your body on the floor or on the chair. Next, imagine yourself in a place where you feel safe and secure — a favorite beach, the mountains, a park, a favorite room. Now, breathe in the pure, fresh air of that place. The air is filled with joy and happiness, so with each breath, take in the joy and well-being of your favorite place and let it fill all the cells of your body. Do this for a few breaths, until your entire body is filled with this sense of joy and purity.

Now take a breath and imagine that you can follow this breath all the way down the left side of your body and down into your left foot. Rest your awareness on your left foot when you get there, from the back of the foot to the tips of the toes and from the top of the foot to the arch and the sole of your foot. Your attention is not just on the surface of the foot but extends deep into the tissue, down to the bones, ligaments, and tendons of your left foot. With a sense of neutrality, just allow yourself to observe whatever sensation is there right now... and right now... and right now. To do this means coming into contact with any sensation you find and then releasing it to make space for the next sensation ... and the next. This is an ongoing process of contacting and releasing, contacting and releasing, again and again. If you feel no sensation in the left foot at this moment, that is perfectly okay. You do not need to create one. Just notice that there is no sensation at the moment.

With your next inbreath, follow it down the left side of your body until it reaches your lower left leg, from the knee down through the shin and calf and to the ankle. Place all of your attention on your lower left leg. As before, sense this body area from moment to moment, contacting and releasing. Savor each sensation, knowing that a sensation is just that, a sensation, neither innately good nor bad. The colors red and tan, for example, are not innately good or bad. Neither is a taste, such as sweet or sour, good or bad; it is just that flavor. In this same way, see if you can just notice the feeling of a sensation before your mind jumps in with a name for it.

After sensing the lower left leg, continue in the same way to bring attention to the upper left leg, the left hand, the left arm, the back and torso (including the inner organs, such as the liver, kidneys, stomach, heart, and lungs), the neck and shoulders, and the face and skull. Then you can move down the body's right side, placing your awareness on the upper right arm, the lower right arm, the right hand, the upper right leg, the lower right leg, and finally the right foot. In this way, you have directed your attention up one side of the body and down the other. You can also experiment with sensing other body parts — such as the ankle, the shin, the knee, the hip — or with combining parts of the body in ways that feel right for you.

I consider the following practices optional because past trauma or injury can make these difficult for some. You do not have to try what follows, but should you want to include any with your body scan, read on.

After scanning and sensing your body, you can reflect on any or all of the following: gratitude, healing, and forgiveness. Let's focus first on gratitude and use the right hand as an example. After you have sensed your right hand, you will spend a few moments reflecting on what your right hand has done for you today. Has it helped you take a shower? Did it help you get dressed? Did it help you make or eat breakfast? Did it help you operate and steer your car? Maybe it gave someone a hug? Send your deep appreciation to your right hand now for tirelessly following your commands without complaint. Smile inwardly at your right hand, letting it know that you are grateful for its efforts to make your life easier and that you care enough to take care of it. In this same way, you can send your healing smile and appreciation to any part of the body.

Should you decide to focus on healing and forgiveness, try the following. While sensing any body part that may be injured, take a moment to send it your healing intention. Do this by inhaling and imagining a white or golden light coming in from the crown of your head. Picture the healing light flowing into the injured body part. You might also visualize this light creating space around the pain or injury. As you exhale, imagine this light flushing away the tension, tightness, and impurities in that body part. Visualize the impurities being drawn down through the body and released out the bottom of your feet, to be sent into the earth for composting. With each exhalation, let that body part relax a little bit more. You can also state your mental intention: May this part of the body be healed and work in harmony and balance with the rest of my body as it was intended to be.

Finally, if you feel that you may have caused harm to a body part, intentionally or unintentionally, you can ask forgiveness and state your intention to take better care of your body in the future. When you are finished, exhale, and as you exhale, release your attention on this part of the body.

The entire Cosmic Smile can take from twenty to thirty minutes, but you can just as easily adapt it as a one-to-three-minute tonic by mentally scanning and smiling at each body part quickly. Here is a strategy for using the Cosmic Smile on a daily basis:

Try making the Cosmic Smile the first thing you do upon waking up in the morning. This can shift your day toward thankfulness and away from worrisome, judgmental thinking. If you feel depressed or anxious, do this for one week and see how it makes you feel.

Notes

Epigraph. John O'Donohue, *Eternal Echoes: Celtic Reflections on Yearning to Belong* (New York: Harper Perennial, 2002), pp. 176–77.

18. Walk When You Walk, Sit When You Sit

I'm not afraid of dying. I just don't want to be there when it happens.

— WOODY ALLEN

$\mathcal{A}$ WOMAN HEARD ABOUT MINDFULNESS and was intrigued. When she learned about a nearby mindfulness center, she went there and asked if she could observe the students for a day. While taking calls on her cell phone and listening to music on her iPod, she also took notes as she moved about the center, from its classrooms to the lounge and the cafeteria. At day's end, she asked someone if she could speak to the head teacher. The teacher consented and asked the woman, "How may I help you?"

"I've been watching your mindfulness teachings all day, and I have a question for you."

The head teacher said nothing. He simply nodded and smiled.

"Well," she continued impatiently, reviewing her note pad, "I notice that your students walk, they sit, they eat, and they read. The fact is, I do all those same things at home. So I really don't get what's so special about this thing called mindfulness that you're teaching here."

"You are correct that you do all the same activities," answered the teacher. "But there may be one important difference. When we walk, we walk. When we sit, we sit. When we eat, we eat. We bring full presence of mind and body together with whatever it is we are doing."

The woman started to say something, but her cell phone rang. Before she could answer it, the teacher winked, "And we don't multitask."

Mindfulness is portable. Today I am sharing the portable teaching in Los Angeles at an art center. Iconic potter Beatrice Wood's distinctive and graceful earthen shapes glow under soft lighting. A diverse group assembles around a long oak table for a reading and a lesson in mindful walking. After I explain some of the basics of mindful walking, a man raises his hand and identifies himself as Ben.

"I've got a simple question. Maybe it's because I'm an engineer," he says, "but why in the world would I want to learn how to walk when I already know how to?" Ben is in his sixties, and he is obviously a no-nonsense kind of guy. He pushes his thick, black-rimmed glasses back up his nose as he waits for my answer and appears to be prepared for a challenge.

"Mindful walking is really about being present," I answer. To describe more fully what I mean, I quote Henry David Thoreau in his essay "Walking": "But it sometimes happens that I cannot easily shake off the village. The thought of some work will run in my head, and I am not where my body is — I am out of my senses. . . . What business have I in the woods, if I am thinking of something out of the woods?"[1]

I then piggyback on Thoreau's question by asking one of my own: "Do you know how many times a baby falls down when it's learning how to walk?" I go on to tell the group that each of us falls approximately ten thousand times when attempting to walk, each time learning more and refusing to give up. But once we've mastered walking, we easily revert to automatic pilot. Yes, it is true you are walking, but you've long since forgotten what it means to really walk, as you once did. When you move quickly, you can stay upright because of the gyroscopic effect. But slow down, and you will become more aware of walking in the here and now. As a wise man once said, "You know you're ready for mindful walking when you're ready to stop your running."

Mindful walking uses the basic three-step mindfulness method to blend the mind and body into harmony. The three-step method involves setting intention, taking action, and using attention to sustain observation. This means you (1) set an intention (such as taking a step with your right leg), (2) follow through with an action (taking that step), and (3) observe what occurs (including physical movements and mental thoughts and perceptions).

Mindful walking is a practice in both mindfulness and meditation because it requires being in the present moment while making something (walking) the focus of sustained attention, just as you learned to do with the breath earlier. As with any sustained-focus exercise, your mind will naturally go elsewhere; this is normal. Each time this happens, gently bring your mind and body back to the three steps: intention, action, and observation. This may feel unnatural at first, especially because it will slow you down. You might also find your body does not balance easily. If you find it easier to mindfully walk without shoes, do this on an appropriate surface. You can begin your mindfulness walking practice at home on a level surface, but in the long run it is ideal for getting present wherever you happen to be — walking up a flight of stairs, entering that office meeting, or walking from the car to get somewhere else.

Begin by setting the intention to take a step with the right foot. As you do, feel the movement of your leg, hip, and foot. Feel and observe your foot as it touches the ground. Next, set the intention to take a step with the left foot. Take several steps this way, repeating the intention with every step you take. Once this begins to feel comfortable, you will move on by adding another intention for each step.

Next, use two different intentions for each step you take. First, set the intention to raise your right foot as you take a step. Then, set the intention to lower your right foot. Feel how your foot and leg rise from the ground, and notice how the heel touches the ground. What part of the foot touches the floor first? Breathe normally as you walk. When you feel comfortable with this level of the practice, you will add a third intention for each step. In addition to the intention to raise and lower your foot, you will add the intention to move your foot forward through the air. Notice how your knee moves with each forward movement. Also, notice how your clothes feel as they move with your leg's forward movement.

The last intention (which brings a total of four intentions for each step) is stated just after you have lowered your foot to the floor. Here you add the intention to shift the weight onto this foot and leg. Notice which muscles loosen and which tighten as you transfer your weight from one side of the body to the other. How is the weight spread throughout your grounded foot? Does your knee flex or tighten? There are now four distinct intentions for each step: raise the foot, move it forward, lower it to the floor, and shift weight to that foot. Continue to walk like this, sustaining attention on all movements. When thoughts arise, just move your awareness back to the intention, action, and observation of walking.

You can also set an intention when you need to turn your body. Set the intention to turn as you make the adjustments necessary to mindfully move in a different direction. The effect is much like taking multiple snapshots of one moment, experiencing each with full attention and clarity.

Any time you apply mindfulness to a movement, you break habitual body movements and addictive patterns by shifting attention to the present moment, thereby retraining the body and mind circuitry. This same basic technique of mindfulness when walking can be applied to other daily activities, such as sitting, cooking, eating, and so on. You can also employ real-time and real-speed mindfulness, which means being mindful with movements at a normal pace. To do this, try walking at a normal or a brisk pace without multitasking. Stay with the overarching intention of walking. Observe all your movements as you move, letting your repeated intention keep you centered on the action.

Use mindful walking during times of transition. Transition often brings uncertainty, which can increase stress. Let yourself walk with total bodily grace, joy, and awareness — as the heroes of the movie *Independence Day* did when they strutted confidently and triumphantly through the desert landscape after saving humankind. Any mindful movement can help you to recall the body's innate dignity, balance, and beauty.

Notes

Epigraph. Eric Lax, *Conversations with Woody Allen: His Films, the Movies, and Moviemaking* (New York: Random House, 2007), p. 84.

1.   Henry David Thoreau, *Walden and Other Writings* (Boston: Adamant Media, 2000), p. 628.

19. Recharge Your Batteries with Sleep

*It is a common experience that a problem difficult at night is resolved
in the morning after the committee of sleep has worked on it.*

— JOHN STEINBECK

THE AVERAGE AMERICAN has a yearly sleep deficit of
anywhere from two hundred to five hundred hours. A
National Sleep Foundation poll found that the percentage of
people sleeping eight hours or more a night on weekdays
dropped from 38 percent in 1998 to 26 percent in 2005.[1] Adults
are not the only ones who are sleepless in America. More and
more children, from middle school to high school, are using
caffeinated energy drinks (now a $5 billion-dollar-a-year in-
dustry) to stay alert. But according to the American Academy
of Sleep Medicine, school-age children need to get ten to eleven
hours of sleep each night.

Not only is sleep as necessary for survival as air and food,
but it is also vital in order for learning to effectively occur in our
brain. The body also requires sleep for healing and well-being.
It takes only three days of reduced sleep to put your body into

a state of chronic stress. Of course, a continued presence of stress hormones compromises the immune system and upsets the body's balance. Lack of sleep also triggers complex metabolic changes linked with food cravings and obesity. One scientific study found, for example, that those who slept fewer than five hours a night weighed significantly more than those who slept more than eight hours — a difference caused by the change in the hormones that regulate appetite and metabolism.[2] Other studies have found that reduced sleep is associated with an increase in child obesity. When we are unable to sleep, our body shares important messages about its inability to experience balance and peace.

I see many clients who struggle with sleep. Sometimes bad habits are the cause: TV in the bedroom, too much caffeine, alcohol, and a racing mind are among such habits. Caffeine, for example, has a long half-life while the liver metabolizes it, which means that caffeine ingested in the morning may remain in the body for up to thirty-six hours. And not only does it stimulate us but it also binds to a receptor in the brain that fools the body into thinking it is not tired. But we can only withdraw from our sleep bank's ATM for so long before our body will demand repayment for nonsufficient sleep funds.

The human body is attuned to sunlight. Our biological rhythms are naturally regulated by darkness, a time when melatonin increases and we become sleepy. The artificial brightness created from televisions, cell phones, and computers interrupts the body's innate sleep mechanisms. Unless you suffer from sleep apnea or another medical issue, your body will sleep when you assist it. It is important, though, not to try too hard or to force your body to sleep because the increased mental effort just makes the mind more active and sleep more elusive. Trust that your body will come back to center over time. Have patience as you retrain your body and restore your balance with sleep.

Do you have a mindful sleep ritual that you do each night to prepare for a good night's sleep? Athletes routinely report having rituals that help them before games, such as stretching, eating the right kind of food, and mental imaging. You may already have a morning ritual before you head out for work, something like showering, getting dressed, eating, saying goodbye to family or pets, and so on. We often overlook the power a conscious ritual has to provide centering and calm. A mindful sleep ritual might mean you spend anywhere from fifteen minutes to an hour preparing for sleep, slowly winding down the day's hectic pace and allowing your mind and body to relax.

It is often a good idea to start a bedtime ritual at the same time each night. This might begin with turning off the TV, computer, phone, or other electronic devices. Turning off the lights simulates the setting of the sun. A cup of chamomile tea or warm milk can signal that this is a time to honor the body with compassion. A warm bath, soothing music, or reading something that is comforting may be an option as well. Exercise can help sleep as long as it isn't done within two hours of bedtime, because exercise stimulates the body.

Sleep is not a multitasking activity, which means you should regard your bedroom as a sacred sleep space. If you wake up during the night, sleep experts recommend leaving the bedroom to read or to do something else that isn't too stimulating. Once you feel sleepy, return to the bedroom. Also, make sure the bedroom is dark. Light streaming in through the windows from streetlights, for example, can affect quality of sleep.

What if you have a racing mind that just won't stop worrying about all those little problems waiting for you the next day? As part of your sleep ritual, you may want to place a pad of paper next to the bed so you can write down all those thoughts. Knowing that you have recorded them for reflection the next day can help to ease their grip on your mind so that you can surrender to sleep. If you get anxious about not being able to sleep at any time during the night, try using your awareness to loosen anxious thoughts while breathing diaphragmatically. Sometimes it can be helpful to choose a calming word or phrase to repeat with each breath, such as "quiet mind," "restful sleep," or "one," to repeat with each breath, replacing the thoughts of a racing mind.

No matter how imbalanced your sleeping pattern may be, you can recover balance. I once worked with a former methamphetamine addict, Barry, who had gone almost two years without sleeping in the evening. He used drugs at night and slept fitfully, if at all, when the sun came up. Barry was so ashamed of his substance abuse that when he did sleep, he would often hide in heating vents or other unconventional places where no one might see him and possibly link his weird sleeping patterns with drug use. Barry's sleep ritual became an essential aspect of his recovery. It took almost a year to retrain his body to sleep through the entire night. For Barry, sleep represented a return to normalcy, to functioning as a real person again. It also became a form of discipline contributing to his confidence to maintain a job and expand his life in new and satisfying ways.

Here is a helpful strategy for recharging your batteries with sleep:

Use visualization to deal with racing thoughts and worries. As you relax using the diaphragmatic breath, imagine a large container into which you place all your worries, anxieties, and concerns. After you have put all troublesome thoughts in the container, picture yourself closing it and putting a lock on it. Before putting the container away, ask yourself one more time: Is there anything else I need to place in the container? If so, place that additional thought in the container. Now you are ready to move the container to a place far, far away from you. You may want to put it behind a brick wall, at the bottom of the ocean, or on the dark side of the moon. Before locking the container, ask yourself for the final time: Is there anything else I need to place in the container? After placing any last thoughts in the container, lock it shut. You can always get to the container if you have to, but know that for now you have stored away all thoughts and concerns, which can wait for tomorrow.

Notes

Epigraph. John Cook, Steve Deger, and Leslie Ann Gibson, *The Book of Positive Quotations* (Minneapolis: Fairview Press, 2007), p. 315.

1.   National Sleep Foundation, "2005 Sleep in America Poll," p. 7, kintera.org/atf/cf/%7BF6BF2668A1B44FE88D1AA5D39340D9CB %7D/2005_summary_of_findings.pdf (accessed June 2009).

2.   Shahrad Taheri, Ling Lin, Diane Austin, Terry Young, and Emmanuel Mignot, "Short Sleep Duration Is Associated with Reduced Leptin, Elevated Ghrelin, and Increased Body Mass Index," *Public Library of Science Medicine* 1, December 7, 2004.

20. Reenvision Your Body's Pain

Events may create physical pain, but they do not in themselves create suffering. Resistance creates suffering. . . . The only problem in your life is your mind's resistance to life as it unfolds.

— DAN MILLMAN

IN THE FILM *The Matrix*, Keanu Reeves's character, Neo, fights against the ubiquitous and seemingly invincible Agent Smith, a sentient computer program whose job is to keep humans from awakening and escaping the false reality into which they have been imprisoned. For those humans caught in the Matrix who believe Agent Smith and the world of the Matrix to be real, his computer-generated bullets are lethal. It is only at the end of the story, after Neo shatters this belief system and literally peers inside Agent Smith and the Matrix, that Neo is freed from fear and able to conquer Agent Smith. Neo discovers that Smith is not as solid, substantial, and menacing a force as he had imagined.

In some ways, Agent Smith is a lot like pain when it takes over our lives; we give it a lot more control over our lives than it deserves. We likely have old and unconscious belief systems about pain that allow it to limit and imprison us. But like Neo, each of us has the ability to generate new awareness and mental states that can alter how we perceive and experience pain.

Shortly after returning to New York from an overseas trip, Norman started to experience malaise. A middle-aged man, a highly active person, and an avid tennis player, Norman was alarmed to find his symptoms worsening into joint stiffness and a full body ache. He saw his doctor, who took blood tests with ominous results. Norman's sedimentation rate, measuring nonspecific inflammation, was far above normal. When his sedimentation rate elevated beyond 115 — usually a sign of critical illness — Norman was admitted to the hospital. His condition did not improve, and to make matters worse, he was unhappy about the amount of blood being drawn from him daily, the hospital diet of processed foods, and what seemed like unnecessary exposure to X-rays during testing. A team of doctors diagnosed Norman with a connective tissue disease in the family of rheumatic and arthritic illnesses.

Within days, his symptoms grew debilitating. In Norman's own words, "I had considerable difficulty moving my limbs and even turning over in bed. Nodules appeared on my body, these gravel-like substances under my skin, which showed the systemic nature of the disease. At the low point of my illness, my jaws were almost locked."[1] One specialist who considered the prognosis grim offered Norman a slim one-in-five-hundred chance for total recovery. Norman, however, did not automatically and mindlessly buy into the prognosis. "Up to that time,

I had been more or less disposed to let the doctors worry about my condition. But now I felt a compulsion to get into the act. It seemed clear to me that if I was to be that one in five hundred, I had better be something more than a passive observer."[2]

Norman spent a lot of time reflecting on how his trip abroad had exposed his body to toxic levels of stress, as well as some harmful environmental pollutants. Based on the big picture rather than just individual symptoms, Norman developed his own diagnosis of endocrine system exhaustion and adrenal gland dysfunction. It dawned on him that maybe he could reverse the insults done to his body and mind, both nutritionally and emotionally.

Back in 1964, the year when Norman became ill, mainstream medicine did not fully acknowledge the harmful effects of stress and negative emotions on the body. Norman came up with a plan for vitamin supplements that his primary physician agreed could not hurt him. Perhaps more importantly, his doctor showed support and excitement for Norman's belief that if negative emotions could cause harm to the body, positive emotions might be able to catalyze the body's healing. By sharing Norman's hope, the doctor opened wider the door of possible recovery. Bolstered by his doctor's support, Norman went into immediate action. "Even before we had completed arrangements for moving out of the hospital, we began the part of the program calling for the full exercise of the affirmative emotions as a factor in enhancing body chemistry," Norman explains.[3]

Norman initiated a regimen of watching funny movies as a way to alleviate his pain. Watching the witty, silly, and irreverent antics of the Marx Brothers and other comedians actually worked! Norman discovered that "ten minutes of genuine belly laughter had an anesthetic effect and would give me at least two hours of pain-free sleep."[4] Norman tested his sedimentation rate before and after laughter, and he found that it would drop slightly after each dose of humor. Soon, the gravel-like nodules began to shrink, mobility slowly returned, and Norman was hopeful that he would survive. There was one negative side effect, however: the laughter and movies kept nearby patients in the hospital up at night!

Norman Cousins's search for healing and health altered the direction of his life in ways he could never have predicted. He uprooted his family and left his career in New York as an editor for *Saturday Review* to work instead as an adjunct professor at the UCLA School of Medicine. By initiating cutting-edge research in the field of mind-body medicine, he influenced a new generation of doctors and healers. His difficult initiation and rite of passage through illness led him into a lifelong exploration of the connection between such things as humor, joy, hope, happiness, and the ability of positive emotions to positively influence body chemistry. Cousins became a respected researcher who bridged the gap between traditional medicine and a growing awareness of the impact mental states have on health.

But that's only half of the story. As Norman Cousins suspected, humor significantly boosts levels of endorphins and human growth hormone, two beneficial regulators of the body's immune system. New research continues to provide positive results about laughter's impacts on our mental and physical health. Dr. Lee Berk, an assistant professor of family medicine at the University of California Irvine College of Medicine, studies the effects of humor on the body and with his colleagues has found that simply informing individuals they will watch a funny video stirs anticipation in them, which elevates their mood states. After actually watching the humorous video, research participants were tested for the stress hormones cortisol, epinephrine, and DOPAC. Researchers found a notable decrease in all of them.[5]

In another study, Berk used therapeutic laughter with a group of high-risk diabetes patients. The control group received standard care, while the experimental group viewed thirty minutes of self-selected humor in addition to receiving standard care. After following both groups for twelve months, Berk learned that the experimental group members showed significantly lower stress hormones than the control group showed. The experimental group also showed a 26 percent increase in good (HDL) cholesterol, compared to only a 3 percent HDL increase in the control group.[6] A growing body of research continues to demonstrate that mental state affects the body. As for laughter, research also shows that the effects of humor last far beyond the time it is first experienced and that it helps to laugh aloud. So let yourself enjoy and savor moments of levity.

To reframe pain through a more hopeful lens, try the following exercise.

Make a list of goals, the things you want to accomplish in life even though you are presently in pain. This list might be different from your pain-free goals list, but that doesn't mean these goals can't be important and satisfying for you. Also, remember that goals can be small things, such as taking a short walk, pursuing a hobby, or seeing the sunset.

Notes

Epigraph. Steve Ryals, *Drunk with Wonder* (Ukiah, CA: Rock Creek Press, 2006), p. 265.

1. Norman Cousins, *Anatomy of an Illness as Perceived by the Patient: Reflections on Healing and Regeneration* (New York: W. W. Norton, 2001), p. 33.

2. Ibid., p. 33.

3. Ibid., p. 43.

4. Ibid., p. 43.

5. Lee S. Berk, "Mind, Body, Spirit: Exploring the Mind, Body, and Spirit Connection through Research on Mirthful Laughter," in *Spirituality, Health, and Wholeness: An Introductory Guide for Healthcare Professionals*, ed. Siroj Sorajjakool and Henry Lamberton (New York: Routledge, 2004).

6. American Physiological Society, "'Mirthful Laughter,' Coupled with Standard Diabetic Treatment, Raises Good Cholesterol and May Lower Heart Attack Risk," press release, www.the-aps.org/press/releases/09/14.htm (accessed December 21, 2009).

21. Let Go of Cravings

A good runner leaves no tracks.

— LAO TZU

CRAVING TAKES MANY FORMS. It can pull us toward something, or it can create aversion and push us away. In either case, it can be so strong that it blinds us to what is actually happening right around us. A problem with craving is that when you give in to it, the craving does not disappear. It is only silenced for a time and then it returns. This cycle can create exhaustion and hopelessness. But with mindfulness, craving doesn't have to blindly lead us where we do not want to go. When you engage your awareness, craving can become an ally of insight.

Craving is certainly one of the causes of suffering in our world. Grasping traps us because it severely narrows our focus until we can see only that one thing we badly want and desire. When we are stuck in grasping, we need to locate the broader, mindful view. This is illustrated in the example of monkeys who cling to food they find in a gourd even when clinging prevents them from eating or freeing themselves. Food is placed in a hollowed-out gourd, but the gourd's opening is barely large enough for a monkey's hand to reach inside, so that once a monkey grasps the food with a clenched fist, it cannot extract its hand. The monkey is stuck. The monkey *could* get unstuck by letting go, but the iron grip of craving holds it in place. This is a powerful metaphor for our own "stuckness," when a craving is so strong and powerful that we feel we can't let go of it. In addition to feeling stuck, we likely experience feelings of helplessness and hopelessness. Craving can make anyone ask, "Is it really possible to be free?" Fortunately, we can learn what a monkey caught in a trap does not know: that the secret to getting free is experiencing the craving and then learning to let it go.

Here is a two-part mindfulness meditation for making craving an ally. The first part will help you to physically experience the power of your craving before releasing some of the energy that binds you. I call this expanding the mindful view, a process by which we can understand craving and get closer to the freedom of the present moment.

Close your eyes for a moment and visualize your craving. Whatever it may be, picture it being located in a gourd like the one that traps monkeys. Now extend your arm and squeeze your hand through the gourd's narrow hole. Let your hand grab and literally clench your craving. However tightly you are holding it, clench it tighter! Keep holding on to it, even if your hand starts feeling fatigued. Observe that this is how it feels to clench and hold on to craving. Feel how painful it is to hold on like this. Let yourself experience how craving is constricting and harming your life in the moment.

Now give yourself permission to let go of your craving by relaxing your hand. Spend at least one minute slowly releasing craving. You might say to yourself, "In this moment, I can relax my mind, relax my grasping, relax my hand, and relax my craving." Slowly release your clenched fist. Feel how the blood returns to your hand. Move your fingers and notice how your hand has freedom of movement again. Observe the pleasant sensation that comes from letting go. Now slowly pull back your arm, remove your hand from the monkey trap, and leave your craving behind for the moment.

At this time, expand your awareness beyond the craving to the space all around you. You can expand the mindful view by paying attention to the moment-by-moment feelings in your body, taking slow, conscious breaths, noticing the different colors in the room, listening to all the sounds around you, or noticing what aromas are present. Observe how the craving can still be present in the gourd, but you do not have to reach inside to grab it. You can be centered and grounded in a mindful view. Also, remember that craving can be the impulse to push something away. Those struggling with anorexia, social anxiety, or fear suffer from a craving in the form of avoidance. These experiences can also be imagined in the gourd. Regardless of how large or small the craving, you can use this meditation to physically observe what it feels like to let go of craving.

The second part of this meditation is based on the idea of "urge surfing," a term coined by psychologist Alan Marlatt.[1]

When caught in the grip of craving, you can surf along with it and ride it out with curiosity and observation. What does it feel like in each moment? You can ride craving's waves without trying to control, eliminate, or give in to them. Instead, you notice that you can fully experience the craving without having to act on it. Feeling and surfing your craving will not harm you. Like ocean waves, cravings rise up and subside into the surf. At times, the surf is restless; other times, it barely creates a ripple. The more you surf your cravings and urges, the more you'll understand how your cravings come and go, as well as become more comfortable with them. What's important is to recognize that you don't need to eliminate the voice of craving within you; you can skillfully decide simply to observe rather than follow it.

Here is another strategy for releasing cravings:

Start to notice the voice and the inexhaustible cravings of your hungry ghost, the part of you that never seems to be satisfied. In Tibetan Buddhism, the hungry ghost is depicted with a large mouth, a long and slender neck, and a giant belly, so the hungry ghost can never swallow enough to satisfy it. Make a list of your cravings, taking care to notice the judgmental mind as you do so. Know that the inner craver is emotionally needy, and be compassionately present for the needy part. It exists in all of us. As you become more aware of what your inner craver desires and truly needs, you can identify better ways to get those needs met.

Notes

Epigraph. R. B. Blakney, *The Way of Life* (New York: Signet Classics, 2001), p. 79.

1. G. Alan Marlatt and Dennis M. Donovan, eds., *Relapse Prevention: Maintenance Strategies in the Treatment of Addictive Behaviors* (New York: Guilford Press, 2007), p. 15.

22. Mind Your Body

The truth of the matter is that even though there are teachings
and practice techniques, still we each have to find our own way.

— PEMA CHÖDRÖN

*I*T SEEMS SO IRONIC TO SPEND A LIFETIME caring for the
body — its arms, legs, eyes, ears, mouth, and so on — because it is designed to slowly fall apart and ultimately fail. And
yet we care for the body and tend to it because it carries wisdom
and knowledge. It is a repository for holding and touching the
present moment. It is our means for finding joy and reaching
out to the world. It is a marvelous instrument, as impermanent
as it is. This last body key strategy emphasizes the preciousness
and uniqueness of your body. Even when being mindful of the
body's struggle — because of trauma, pain, or some other reason — you can simply mind the body as it is.

It is a brisk and sunny day in Portland as I prepare to teach a
class with classically trained French chef Robert Reynolds.

Chef Robert will lead the class in mindful food preparation and cooking, and I will teach mindful eating. Before we enter the kitchen, Chef Robert tells the class how the French train children to enjoy food and to be discriminating from a very young age. He describes how the French, like many peoples, take a long break in the middle of the workday to return home, be with the family, and prepare a meal from scratch — with mindful preparation and appreciation of the ingredients. At one point, Chef Robert carefully picks up an onion, cradles it in his hands, and with a twinkle in his eye says, "The French will look at an onion, and say, 'God created you as perfect; now what can I do to add to this perfection?'"[1]

And indeed, Chef Robert cradles all food with attention and love. With his guidance, the class prepares an easy creamy sauce for a simple yet elegant meal of tilapia and asparagus. They cook carrots and red bell peppers with the skin peeled off, and then blend them until they are the perfect consistency. Only then do they add any seasonings. According to Chef Robert, you need to do one thing at a time, first paying attention to the consistency and then putting full attention on the seasoning. The art of cooking, as well as the art of living, is best done lovingly, slowly, and moment to moment.

To enlighten the body means appreciating and connecting with the body by taking the attitude that "God created you as perfect." (I doubt that any onion, tomato, or olive would consider itself inferior to another.) This is what Father Thomas Merton meant when he wrote, "The more a tree is like itself, the more it is like Him. . . . This particular tree will give glory to God by spreading out its roots in the earth and raising its branches into the air and the light in a way that no other tree before or after it ever did or will do."[2] To know this is to connect to the inner wisdom of mindfulness.

If you find this too difficult, you can just rest in what the body does. Thich Nhat Hanh speaks to this when he says, "There are two ways to wash the dishes. The first is to wash the dishes in order to have clean dishes and the second is to wash the dishes in order to wash the dishes."[3] Which of these ways would you choose? Which do you choose?

No one is saying you have to love your body in order to be mindful. You can hate it if you want and still be mindful, but that emotion will not be beneficial to you or your life. Maybe you can settle into knowing that this body is yours to mind and that you can mind it to the best of your ability — one mindful step at a time, one washed dish at a time, one simple breath at a time. With the body key teachings, you have already taken several steps on the journey of increasing body awareness and inhabiting the moment with openness and acceptance. Integrate these teachings. Bring them into your life, and you will find new treasures of joy and fulfillment await you.

Here is an overall means for applying the body key teachings:

Review the body key teachings and see which one you could most benefit from at this time. Commit to using this single practice on a daily basis, whether it is breathing, the Cosmic Smile, or letting go of cravings. After practicing for one week, move on to another body key teaching you feel will benefit you, and use it for an entire week. Find ways of adapting each practice so that it fits into your day. What's important is that each teaching becomes part of, not separate from, how you naturally spend your time.

Notes

Epigraph. Pema Chödrön, *Start Where You Are: A Guide to Compassionate Living* (Boston: Shambhala, 2001), p. 52.

1. Mindful Eating — Mindful Cooking Class, March 3, 2007, Portland, Oregon.

2. Thomas Merton, *New Seeds of Contemplation* (New York: New Directions Publishing, 1972), p. 29.

3. Thich Nhat Hanh, *The Miracle of Mindfulness* (Boston: Beacon Press, 1987), p. 4.

PART THREE
THE SPIRIT KEY

*T*HE SPIRIT KEY TEACHINGS ILLUSTRATE how to touch the present moment by finding deeper meaning and purpose. We need to understand how to unlock the code of the spirit to feel fulfilled and to grasp our place in the cosmos. With each spirit key, may you discover that unlocking this code is easier than you might imagine.

23. Connect to Nature's Source

Look deep into nature, and then you will understand everything better.

— ALBERT EINSTEIN

ONE OF THE GREAT CHALLENGES of this modern age is learning how to set boundaries around technology. According to a 2009 survey on traffic safety by the AAA Foundation, one in five persons texts or emails while driving a car.[1] Although technology can be highly beneficial, it's important to understand that when we plug in 24/7, we easily become robotic ourselves and neglect the vital, intimate, and nourishing connection to what is natural within ourselves and the world we inhabit. We risk losing all that an inner stillness and nature have to offer us.

This morning I visit with a young man whose complexion resembles the pasty shade of plaster. He trundles slowly into my counseling office like a gadget whose batteries are going dead. His light green eyes make contact for only a sliver of a second before his head tilts back down, as if it were attached to an unseen counterweight. His untamed, dark brown hair curls tightly this way and that over his forehead, ears, and neck. When I shake his hand, I feel flesh and fingers that are cold and almost devoid of energy. Over the next hour, I learn more about Roy, a seventeen-year-old whose desperate mother had initially called to see if I could help her son improve his schoolwork and prospects for college. I find Roy to be refreshingly honest and forthcoming. He shares with me his sentiment that school is a chore and that he does not like most of his classes and teachers. As we speak, Roy divulges that he spends approximately ten hours a day in his room, sometimes longer, after returning from school.

"What are you doing during all that time?" I ask.

"I'm on the computer," responds Roy, who then describes a daily routine of listening to or downloading music, using graphics programs to create images, instant-messaging friends who are online, surfing the Internet, and sometimes attending to homework assignments, but only those that can be done on the Internet. He also spends time answering cell phone calls, receiving and sending text messages and emails, listening to CDs, and viewing DVD movies or YouTube or MTV clips — all simultaneously.

As Roy talks, his voice eerily reminds me of an automated voicemail system I was trapped in earlier in the week. I feel myself tensing up, and so I pause to take a breath, bringing attention to my posture and observing the soles of my feet pressing on the floor. My mind stops, and for a moment I am just present, not thinking or trying to fix anything. I am simply aware, trying to experience empathy with this young man by looking inside at my own feelings. That's when a strange sense of loss flashes before me. At that instant, a deep sadness wells up within me and a longing for the lost inheritance of what is elemental, natural, and primal — trees, flowers, pollen, sun, wind, rocks, insects, and all those organic connections that help to soothe and reassure an overstimulated brain.

If I were a shaman, I would direct Roy to go to the wilderness and guide him in a vision quest or a similar nature-based rite of passage. I would have him study the works of Lao Tzu, Taoist master from the sixth century BCE, who observed, "Nature does not hurry, yet everything is accomplished."[2] I ask Roy, instead, if he has tried to study and complete his school assignments. The question feels lame and inadequate, and I wonder if it shows on my face, but Roy's expression doesn't change. He reports that he can't concentrate on reading a book for more than a few minutes at a time. I nod my head, knowing that Roy is not alone in having a splintered attention span. There is a small but growing body of evidence indicating that computer multitasking on a daily basis may affect the frontal lobe, causing the brain to lose its capacity for the deep attention and focus required for such things as reading, impulse control, long-term learning, and recognizing facial expressions. For example, a study conducted by Professor Ryuta Kawashima and his team at Tohoku University in Japan mapped the brains of teens who either performed arithmetic or played a Nintendo game. When comparing brain scans, they found that arithmetic stimulated the frontal lobe, while the computer game quieted the frontal lobe, stimulating activity only in the vision and movement parts of the brain.[3] This phenomenon is not just affecting teens.

A British study funded by Hewlett-Packard in 2005 showed a loss in IQ of up to ten points in participants when they juggled work, emails, and other distractions.[4] (This is more than double the loss found in those who smoke marijuana.) Now consider this finding in the context of the more than 36 billion daily emails estimated for 2005 and the messages also cluttering Americans' cell phones.[5] Although it would be simplistic to blame Roy's problems on technology, it would be just as naive to ignore the evidence that our brain structure is shaped by the focus of our attention.

I wish I could say that my meeting with Roy met a successful conclusion, but after that session, I never saw Roy or heard from his mother again. Whatever was wedged between this mother and son never became my work to discover. What their situation did leave me with, however, was another view of multitasking. It's not enough to explain Roy's story, yet it may say something important about a young man and how he copes. Perhaps it's the story of how many of us now cope, live, and interact in an age of industrialization, speed, semipersonal communal technology, and isolation from the natural world and its rhythms. Technology is no longer "out there"; it has become an extension of our very humanity.

And so I wonder: *Will the day come when the wild places that exist within and around our cities slowly disappear? Will we one day cease to seek them out? Will we cease loving them and answering their call? And if wild places disappear, will we ever again discover the wise inner stillness that nature nurtures in us?* Sitting alone in my office after Roy and his mother leave, I listen as the outside door closes and the dangling metal blinds covering it rattle. I recall naturalist John Muir and his understanding of the human need for wild places: "Everybody needs beauty as well as bread, places to play in and pray in, where Nature may heal and cheer and give strength to body and soul alike."[6]

When you feel overwhelmed, stressed, and multitasked to your limit, try the following exercise.

At least once a day, take a purposeful break from multitasking. Stop and take time to notice something new about the natural environment — a flower, a scent, an insect. See how many different shades of green you can distinguish. (The color green actually soothes and calms the brain.) Also, you might find a favorite wild place and want to take its picture, so that you can put it on your screen saver or carry a snapshot of it with you to remind you of your need for what is natural.

Notes

Epigraph. Mark Coleman, *Awake in the Wild: Mindfulness in Nature as a Path of Self-Discovery* (Novato, CA: New World Library, 2006), p. 119.

1. AAA Foundation for Traffic Safety, 2009 Traffic Safety Culture Index, http://www.aaafoundation.org/pdf/2009TSCIndexPR.pdf (accessed August 2009).

2. Lao Tzu, *Tao Teh King*, trans. Archie J. Bahm (Albuquerque: World Books, 1986), p. 91.

3. Tracy McVeigh, "Computer Games Stunt Teen Brains," http://www.guardian.co.uk/world/2001/aug/19/games.schools (accessed December 2009).

4. "Emails 'Hurt IQ More Than Pot,'" http://www.cnn.com/2005/WORLD/europe/04/22/text.iq/ (accessed August 2009).

5. "Email Boxes to Increase to 1.2 Billion Worldwide by 2005," http://archives.cnn.com/2001/TECH/internet/09/19/email.usage.idg/ (accessed December 2009).

6. John Muir, *The Yosemite* (New York: Century Company, 1920), p. 256.

24. Practice Loving-Kindness Toward Yourself

Mindfulness is free. We are born with it.

—— VENERABLE U SILANANDA

*H*AVE YOU EVER MET ANYONE whom you instantly sensed was filled with boundless compassion and kindness? This happened to me when a friend introduced me to the late U Silananda, an unassuming Burmese monk, during a visit to San Francisco. I had been told Silananda was well known for his mindfulness teachings, but what impressed me most about him was the palpable sense of compassion he emanated. Mind you, this wasn't my reaction to a charming smile or an unctuous greeting. I was responding to the deep and abiding peace in his eyes and face. He made me wonder: *How did he become like this? What has he learned that transformed him in this way? Can I learn this? Can others?*

A couple of years after meeting Silananda, I learned that I could be ordained as a Buddhist monk at the monastery in which he was the abbot, or *sayadaw*. I was fortunate to learn mindfulness and other valuable lessons from him, and during my time in the monastery and on meditation retreats, I found he was always teaching the ancient wisdom of loving-kindness. Eventually, I realized that this was what he practiced every day.

What does loving-kindness meditation do? As far as I can tell from personal experience and the experiences others share in their work with me, it soothes the brains of those who have been traumatized — and most of us have been traumatized in one way or another while living on this wounded planet. We might say that loving-kindness acts as a catalyst that alters and reworks the brain's connections and networks from the inside out. It unravels tangled emotions and fears of being hurt and rejected, and then it rewires us with feelings of safety, protection, well-being, and love. In this sense, loving-kindness is as much about receiving love as about giving it. How can we really love others if we do not first genuinely love ourselves? Without such inner hospitality, we will likely push away gifts from others because we are unable to be generous with ourselves. Loving-kindness is inner work. There is no SAT test that can measure our capacity for compassion.

Loving-kindness is also a mind training that helps us grasp the powerful notion that we are not alone in our suffering and pain. It gives us the tools to spread compassion outward, when and where we least expect it. Although the words of the loving-kindness meditation are simple, they powerfully prime the brain and the body for a completely new kind of experience. Loving-kindness is big enough to overcome our smallest and greatest fears. You can imagine the love coming from whatever source you are comfortable with — a prayer, God, or someone you have known. Cultivating loving-kindness is like getting a great big, warm, cosmic hug. This hug can change how you feel each day, so you will want to use it often.

In the next part of this book, "The Relationship Key," I will guide you through an important aspect of loving-kindness meditation that addresses sending loving-kindness to others — but first, I want you to get comfortable as you learn the words. Practice them anywhere and anytime. It helps to find a quiet place at home or in nature where you won't be interrupted.

When you are ready to begin, close your eyes and imagine yourself sitting in a safe and protected place you love. It could be a place on the beach, a location high in the mountains, a favorite park, or a room you like. Picture yourself sitting in that place, and as you do, sense your feet beneath you and your hands in your lap. Let yourself know that the air surrounding you is pure and clean and filled with joy, happiness, and well-being. Breathe in this invigorating pure air, and imagine that its purity, happiness, and well-being reach all the way down through your feet to the tips of your toes. With each new breath, the air fills the cells in your body with purity and joy. Do this until the air penetrates into the cells of your entire being — head, heart, lungs, torso, arms, hands, back, abdomen, legs, and feet. Let it fill your brain too.

Now you will take a few minutes to reflect on forgiveness,

which is important for cultivating the inclusive, nondiscriminating state of loving-kindness. Forgiveness does not mean we forget the wrongs others have done; rather, forgiveness is a gift we give to others and ourselves. After all, haven't we all harmed another at some time, whether intentionally or unintentionally? If you find forgiving certain people difficult and are not ready, this is understandable. Begin then by focusing on those whom you feel you can forgive at this time. While you imagine seeing the individuals you choose, repeat the following words:

May I offer forgiveness to [fill in the name]
As well as to others who may have harmed me —
either intentionally or unintentionally.

May I be forgiven by [fill in the name]
As well as others whom I may have harmed —
either intentionally or unintentionally.

May I forgive myself
for the times that
I may have harmed or abused myself—
either intentionally or unintentionally.

May all beings be forgiven
and find forgiveness.

Then return to your breath, breathing in the joy and happiness of your safe and favorite place. When you feel relaxed and receptive, let yourself sense the deep love you have felt for another, whether a person, a pet, or even a stuffed animal. This is the same feeling of love you will now extend to yourself. If for any reason you feel unworthy of this love, imagine yourself as a small baby, completely deserving of love and caring, as you repeat the loving-kindness blessing. Say the words mentally to yourself repeatedly for at least five minutes, letting the blessing fill every cell and pore of your being. You can also choose to imagine someone else saying these words to you — perhaps a loving grandparent, a caring neighbor, anyone who would show you kindness. You will discover that the blessing is more than just words when you feel yourself opening to the words.

There are different variations of the loving-kindness prayer; I like the following version because it is short and direct. When you have finished, end with a personal blessing of thanks for what you have in your life.

May I be safe,
May I be happy,
May I be healthy,
May I be at peace.

May I be free from pain,
May I be free from hunger,
May I be free from all suffering.

Why send loving-kindness to ourselves before sending it out to others? The first part of the loving-kindness meditation is about receiving the gifts others offer us. How can we give unless we know what it is to receive? And we need to be able to draw from reserves of love within if we want to share with others. This kind of self-regard is not a narcissistic form of love, the me-first or me-only kind of love. This self-regard is the willingness to open and receive the boundless and innate nature of our being, love. It also supports letting go of negative, ego-driven emotions and reactions.

Here is a practical strategy for putting loving-kindness into action.

Make time to do one loving and caring thing for yourself every day. This could be singing a song, getting a massage, or being patient with yourself. Look for ways to compliment yourself too, especially for self-care practices, such as preparing a nourishing breakfast for yourself. Also practice graciously accepting a compliment or gift from another.

Note

Epigraph. U Silananda in conversation with the author, September 1996.

25. Awaken the Tender Heart

*If you search for awakened heart, if you put your hand through your
rib cage and feel for it, there is nothing there except for tenderness.
You feel sore and soft ... because your heart is completely exposed.*

— CHÖGYAM TRUNGPA

WITH MORE THAN 160 WARS in the past century, can we
deny that humans love war? You may not think you personally love war, you may well be opposed to war, but still you
cannot deny times when you yourself were blinded by war and
winning in one of its various forms — fear, greed, intolerance,
impatience, jealousy, envy, lust, ignorance, aggression.

In *A Terrible Love of War*, psychologist James Hillman
writes about the many assumptions we have about the causes
of war. He observes that we have unconsciously accepted war
because it has been woven so deeply into our mythologies,
religions, and prevailing collective psyche. Hillman refers also
to a god of rashness: a god that is unrelenting in its desire for
all that is immediate, fast, and superefficient. And so, we are
left asking: Is it possible to love no-war and no-harm? Is it

possible to locate the tender heart, which feels the preciousness of all life?

In the climax of director Ridley Scott's classic science fiction film *Blade Runner*, the hero Deckard, played by Harrison Ford, faces off against his nemesis Roy, an artificially intelligent, human-type clone replicant, played by Rutger Hauer. The situation looks bleak for Deckard, who dangles helplessly over the edge of the rooftop, clinging to life with mere fingertips. An arrogant expression spreads across Roy's face as he peers down at Deckard. Just when it seems Roy will push Deckard to certain death, Roy does something extraordinary. He reaches down and with his superhuman strength lifts the exhausted Deckard onto the roof. When Roy divulges extraordinary details of his life, Deckard's facial expressions change from surprise to uncertainty to the dawning of a deeper understanding of and even tenderness and empathy for his foe. Even though he has been genetically designed to live for a predetermined time and is within minutes of expiring, Roy saves Deckard. Although he spent his life warring on behalf of his human masters, Roy's final urge is not to fight but to transcend his programming and find meaning in his story. One could say he experiences a state of no-war within.

Not unlike Roy, real-life Englishman John Newton lived a life of violence that began at a young age. His mother died when he was six, and when he was eleven, he was taken off to be raised at sea by his father, a rough-and-tumble sailor. At age nineteen, John was a troubled young man who deserted the navy and was sent to the brig for his transgression. He was released from the brig only because he agreed to sign a contract to work for a violent and ruthless ship captain. John's life appears dismal and hopeless even in this sanitized version of his story.

John was born in the 1700s. He did not willingly enlist in the British navy; he was kidnapped and forced to serve. The contract that released him from the brig made him an indentured servant of an abusive captain, and the ship he was forced to work on was not just any commercial ship but a slave-trading vessel filled with Africans suffering unimaginable indignities and abuse. Luckily, a friend of John's father helped to save John from toiling on the slave ship. But as harsh as John Newton's world was, it was a world he knew well, which may be why he ended up commanding his own slave ship in the mid-1700s. John became so fierce a commander that once when he fell overboard, his crew refused to lower a boat. They threw a harpoon at him instead and towed him back as he clung to it.

In this unlikely setting, while plying the most wretched of trades and carrying as many as six hundred persons on the slave ship *Greyhound*, John discovered his tender heart. It happened during a terrifying storm when the *Greyhound* seemed about to sink. The livestock were the first to be washed overboard and lost to the dark, roiling sea. The crew desperately lashed themselves to masts and other fixtures to keep themselves from being tossed overboard. All the while, John tried to steer the creaking wooden vessel through one pounding, monstrous wave after another. When all seemed lost, John heard himself cry out, "Lord, have mercy upon us!" After that, he somehow found the strength to navigate through the storm, which thankfully abated. Although the ordeal was past, the shaken ship captain could not get the words "Lord, have mercy upon us" out of his head. He came to realize that he had been touched by grace, that somehow God had spoken to him about the possibility and necessity of living without causing brutality and suffering. Eventually, John Newton left his life as a slave ship captain to become a minister. At the age of fifty-four, he accepted a ministry at St. Mary Woolnoth in London. While writing a sermon one evening, he recalled his lost years as a slave ship captain and penned these words:

> *Amazing Grace, how sweet the sound*
> *That saved a wretch like me,*
> *I once was lost, but now am found,*
> *Was blind, but now I see.*

Later set to music, Newton's "Amazing Grace" remains a testament to how a new understanding and purpose can reorient a hardened human heart toward tenderness and openness. Newton was a minister for more than twenty-five years. The audience for his antislavery writings and personal memoirs grew beyond his church and inspired the British politician William Wilberforce to lead an uphill battle for the abolishment of slavery in Great Britain.

The Dalai Lama once said, "If you can, help and serve other sentient beings; if you cannot, then at least do not harm others."[1]

When your heart softens, it contacts the world with all its sorrows, and you begin to lose the sharp distinctions between yourself and other beings. Just as we need one hand to wash the other, how can we exploit and harm what is so close to us? Realizing this may cause us to cry with sadness at the impermanence and frailty of all life. We may be afraid of this truth. We may not want to let the world touch us for fear of being taken advantage of or abused. But when we don't let the light of tenderness inside, we harm ourselves by building a wall around our heart.

How can we remove the wall? By being aware in the here and now of the violence and aggression that exist within us. Mundane, daily events will reveal this to us — such as the rage that wells up when we hear an opposing view on talk radio or when someone gets in our way on the highway. Maybe your aggression button gets pushed when you meet with an inconvenience or another's arrogance, authority, or stupidity. At these pivotal moments, we have a choice: to act selfishly, judgmentally, impatiently, and insensitively, at the expense of another, or to shine the light of our attention on our aggressive thoughts and defuse potential harm. We can dismantle the wall one brick at a time.

The following training builds awareness, compassion, and appreciation for life's tenderness.

Whenever you notice yourself constricting, let yourself soften. You can cultivate softening by noticing the moments when you harden — for instance, when you want to win at all costs, to condemn another, or to get more of a shared resource (energy, food, etc.) than you need. It can help to keep a journal throughout the day. You can short-circuit selfish impulses in the moment by taking a breath and letting generosity fill your heart. Make a point of letting others go in front of you in line, of eating half your meal and giving away the rest, or of giving away something you cherish, such as a book, an item of clothing, or some other valued object. Each time you soften, consider it a gift from others who are helping you learn the joy of altruism and compassion.

Notes

Epigraph. Chögyam Trungpa, *Shambhala: The Sacred Path of the Warrior* (Boston: Shambhala, 1988), p. 45.

1. Dalai Lama, *Live in a Better Way: Reflections on Truth, Love, and Happiness*, ed. Renuka Singh (New York: Penguin, 2002), p. 31.

26. See the Truth of Impermanence

*I*MPERMANENCE IS THE WAY OF THE UNIVERSE. It is evident in the way we breathe air in and out and in the field of gravity, which bends all space, time, and matter, including our small and fragile bodies. Sometimes life presents a change that doesn't seem right or fair, such as an illness, a relationship that ends, death, the loss of a job, bankruptcy, or other calamity. Evidence of aging is usually not a welcome change. Whatever the case, we would like to slay such an evil dragon, to push it away and believe that permanent escape is possible. But there may be another way.

I still remember the conversation I had many years ago with a writer, Fred, who told me he had just received a diagnosis of adult-onset diabetes. "Did your doctor put you on a special diet? What are you going to do?" I inquired. "I'm going to find a new doctor," he answered with a wry laugh. The thing was, Fred wasn't kidding. Such a response of total denial is not unusual. Many headstrong children and adults cling to beliefs regardless of how things might change before their eyes.

Our mind-set around death is one example of a strong cultural belief that disfavors change. We have come to believe that it is more proper to die in a hospital than at home. Death is quickly swept away and sanitized. The U.S. government instituted a no-photo policy of the caskets of American soldiers killed in Iraq. Consider how often bodies are embalmed when they die, as if to continue the illusion of a body that remains intact, without signs of decay, disintegration, or impermanence. In contrast, Tibetans traditionally keep the body of the deceased with the family for several days of prayer and chanting, during which time the body shrinks and decays. It may not be pretty or sanitized, but it is real.

We maintain endless preferences in life — many much less profound than wanting to turn away from death — and we are fiercely attached to some of them. I was quite attached to my hair until I was ordained a monk. Impermanence is the first lesson taught to new monks in the Theravada tradition. After each scrape of the straight razor against my head, a monk held a lock of my cherished hair between his fingers and said to me, "This is not you." When I stopped in the bathroom to wash my face after the initiation ceremony, I was a shocked to see my bald reflection. I wondered who had invited Uncle Fester of *The Addams Family* into the bathroom with me. A bit of my belief in the permanence of the body let go in that moment.

Each attachment makes it harder to let go, to accept the nature of change. But what would life be like if change never took place? How would that girl or boy grow up to be a productive, energetic young adult? Without social change, many of us would be mired in feudalism and slavery. If the autumn leaves didn't fall, there would be no space for spring's buds to take hold. Lightning strikes and causes the forest fire, which supports the natural replenishment of ecosystems. Even our own brain undergoes a process of pruning neural pathways at different stages in our life span to make space for the richness of existing and emerging circuits. Awareness and acceptance of impermanence can liberate the spirit and help us to appreciate the preciousness of life. The more we can create a spaciousness and an acceptance of the temporary nature of all things, the less important our preferences become as well. I am reminded of Sufi poet Rumi's insights in "The Guest House":

> *This being human is a guest house.*
> *Every morning a new arrival.*
>
> *A joy, a depression, a meanness,*
> *some momentary awareness comes*
> *as an unexpected visitor.*
>
> *Welcome and entertain them all!*
> *Even if they're a crowd of sorrows,*
> *who violently sweep your house*
> *empty of its furniture.*
> *Still, treat each guest honorably.*
> *He may be clearing you out*
> *for some new delight.*

The dark thought, the shame, the malice,
meet them at the door laughing,
and invite them in.

Be grateful for whoever comes,
because each has been sent
as a guide from beyond.[1]

Here is a mindful means for opening the door of your guest house to the truth of impermanence.

Make friends with people of all ages, especially the aging and dying. Don't insulate yourself from death and what it means to let go. Practice the exercise of writing your own obituary, and notice your emotions when you do this exercise. When you explore impermanence in this intimate way, you can better evaluate whether you are living a full and joyous life.

Notes

Epigraph. From "Gott spricht zu jedem / God speaks to each of us...,"
    from *Rilke's Book of Hours: Love Poems to God* by Rainer Maria Rilke
    (p. 88), translated by Anita Barrows and Joanna Macy, copyright © 1996
    by Anita Barrows and Joanna Macy. Used by permission of Riverhead
    Books, an imprint of Penguin Group (USA) Inc.

1. "The Guest House," from *The Essential Rumi* by Jalal al-Din Rumi
    (p. 109), translated by Coleman Barks, copyright © 1997 by Coleman
    Barks. Reprinted by permission of Coleman Barks.

27. Appreciate Ordinary Goodness

When you're down, when you don't have your best game going,
just a nod of acknowledgment means the world.

— OPRAH WINFREY

A MAN IS ON THE PHONE WHILE DRIVING. Suited up in his soccer gear, his twelve-year-old son sits quietly next to him in the car. When the car slows down and pulls over by a large grassy field, the man gets off the phone, looks at his son, and then looks at his watch.

"What time will your game be over? I can be back about 5:30," he says.

The boy slowly unbuckles his seat belt and just sits there, obviously upset but not saying a word.

"What? What is it?" says the father impatiently. "I don't have a lot of time."

"When are you going to see me play?"

"I know I said I'd come to a game, but this is a really, really busy and stressful time for me. I promise I'll come to your next game."

"You always say that," says the boy, fighting back the tears and slowly unbuckling his seat belt.

"Look, I'm sorry," sighs his father, "but this time I really mean it. Next game, okay? Promise."

"There is no next game. Today's our last game," the boy says.

The father is shocked and speechless. Until this moment, he has been blind to how his indifference has affected his son. This true story reminds us that although life can be stressful, difficult, and challenging, we need to awaken to how our actions affect others. How do we cultivate a mindful awareness, which allows us to appreciate all the basic goodness that surrounds us each day? To do so would actually give us more of life to celebrate.

This morning I sit in the coffeehouse located just a few miles up a winding road from where I live and notice the pleasing mix of chocolate and mocha colors on the walls around me. Outside, snow falls in silence. The flakes clump together like curled pieces of white confetti, melting when they touch the sidewalk and the street. The sky, lit up brightly with irregular patches of blue earlier this morning, is now blanketed with clouds. The diffuse light from outside spreads across the coffeehouse's concrete floor, which is compactly speckled with browns, blacks, and grays, resembling a Seurat pointillist painting.

Each time the front door opens, I feel the chill air on my skin and hands. Buttoning the top button on my shirt shifts my awareness for a moment; I notice the jeans, the shirt, and the shoes that keep me warm. I even pay attention to the pale yellow chair that comfortably supports my sitting body. The chair's fabric is soft, like velvet, with long and graceful lines of embroidery. My hands and fingertips welcome the warmth from the cup of coffee I hold. Dwelling on that sensation, I slowly raise the cup and feel the hot liquid on the roof of my mouth and taste the sweetness of honey mixing with the coffee's smoky flavor. For some moments, I pause to reflect on the faraway place, high in the mountains of Peru, where these coffee beans were grown and harvested. I wonder how consuming this product connects me, even in a subtle way, with hundreds of people whom I have never met but with whom I share mutual interest. I hear the murmur of intent conversation from various couples. Today happens to be Valentine's Day. A vast range of emotions seems to exist even here in the early morning. I notice some people smiling with joy; others seem to be sharing sadness or heartfelt thoughts, and still others have animated expressions of openness and curiosity.

Suddenly, an unexpected thing — as if from nowhere, a small, round object rolls beside me and plops onto its side. It resembles a gigantic white pill. No one sits near my yellow chair. The closest couple is about ten feet away to my right, far from the direction from which the pill has rolled. Turning my head, I see a little girl playing near her mother at the far end of the space, perhaps forty-five feet away. Has she unknowingly kicked it in my direction? This unexpected appearance of a giant pill makes me chuckle. Leaning down, I pick it up, touching the slightly rough surface. Each side is imprinted with the picture of a single leaf. Closing my eyes, I raise the pill to my nose to discover the subtle and pleasing aroma of mint. Is there a message here for me? If not about my breath, maybe the mint is a metaphor about noticing the sweetness of life? A sign of how easily amused I can be? I take a breath and fill my lungs deeply, noticing how my abdomen rises, then falls. Each breath acts as an anchor that brings me into this moment. This moment is sweet.

Have you ever heard of the Native American ritual tradition known as the Giveaway? The Giveaway helps us to gain a mature perspective on giving by requiring us to give to others and to recognize how much is given to us each day without our even asking. Native Americans regard the buffalo as a Giveaway because all of the animal — its hide, horns, flesh, and bones — is a gift that bears many benefits for others.

If you are being pulled down into the quicksand of not having enough, of wanting more, of focusing on what is missing in your life, pause to consider what we are all given in any moment — the sunlight, which makes life possible; the air we breathe; and for most of us the food we enjoy, access to clean water to replenish our cells, a shelter that protects us from the elements, electricity that gives light and makes many forms of communication possible, educational resources to better our lives, the clothes that keep us warm, the beauty of nature to enrich our lives, and relationships that nourish us. We take so many ordinary good things for granted and tend to overlook how they make life more satisfying. Some people's basic needs are not met, which is also a call not to take what we have for granted and not to waste resources without regard for the consequences. By recognizing what we are given, we practice celebrating the ordinary goodness of life and can become aware of ways in which we can contribute to the ordinary goodness of others.

Here is a three-step strategy for shifting your mindful attention toward gratitude and ordinary goodness.

First, turn your attention to what you have in your life from the very moment you wake in the morning. Appreciate the breath, the blankets that warm you, the shower that refreshes and cleans you, and even the alarm clock that wakes you up. Next, find a reminder of ordinary goodness that you can carry with you throughout the day, such as a picture of a loved one, a stone or other object from a memorable trip, or an inspirational quote. Finally, share your appreciation of ordinary goodness with others. Doing so does not ignore the difficulties of life. Sharing ordinary goodness is about helping one another enjoy that which makes life worthwhile.

Note

Epigraph. Oprah Winfrey and Denzel Washington, "Little Things Matter," *Parade* magazine, www.parade.com/articles/editions/2007/edition _12-16-2007/AOprah_and_Denzel (accessed June 2009).

28. Live Today on Purpose

The old storytellers knew . . . that each of our myths, our sacred secret stories, is the outpouring of deep longing for meaning, which by some still unknown form of alchemy confers purpose to our lives.

— PHIL COUSINEAU

ONE SUMMER'S DAY, WHILE DRIVING along Highway 82 through eastern Oregon's vast, high desert — a rugged and diverse landscape of steep canyons, rolling fields, snow-capped mountains, and cattle ranches — I came upon a road sign unlike any other I had ever seen. This unassuming little sign had an unusual warning: "Control Noxious Weeds. It's Your Responsibility." I've never heard of a weed causing a vehicle crash or impeding a driver's vision, so I wondered what other meanings this road sign held.

Ralph Waldo Emerson wrote, "What is a weed? A plant whose virtues have not yet been discovered."[1] When you think about it, the practice of Intentionally Centering Attention Now is about watching for the mental and emotional weeds that obstruct our view and clarity. Rather than letting those tumbling weeds within us cause an accident, we can choose to see them for what they are. Each weed guides us toward planting a beautiful garden of thoughts. As Emerson points out, weeds have value when we look closely. Can the weeds of your life help you find the life you want?

Human literature and history reflect the basic human need to find purpose. At our core, we are seekers of purpose and meaning. Purpose can motivate us when we feel lost, frozen, or just plain stuck. Sometimes a purpose comprises our basic human needs, such as food, shelter, sex, and companionship. Other times a purpose is a higher purpose that gives meaning and dignity to our lives.

It is important to identify the weeds in our life, those persons, situations, emotions, events, and moments that cause us to feel discouraged, unappreciated, helpless, or worthless. A purpose transforms these weeds into a beautiful blossom of rebirth and renewal. If your purpose, for example, is to care for your family, then what might be experienced as an unsatisfying job becomes a gift because it allows you to fulfill your purpose. Most jobs involve giving something to another, which can be viewed as a higher purpose. Waitresses "serve," or give energy, on behalf of customers. Truck drivers move products to those who benefit from them. With such a perspective, the work you do on a daily basis becomes an act of giving, which can be your purpose. This means not that you would never want to find another job, one that may hold greater meaning or satisfaction for you, but rather that it's possible to find purpose in what you are already doing.

Purpose is not a magician's trick or an illusion meant to keep you from experiencing the realities of life. Purpose is more like a compass that helps you navigate the difficult roads of life, preventing you from getting so lost that you're unable to find the way back home. How do you find such a compass? You can follow the advice of author and mythologist Joseph Campbell to follow one's bliss. Identifying our passion, or bliss, is a good way to discover purpose. Following our passion can also carry us through times of hardship. Nelson Mandela had a purpose that sustained him, keeping his spirit strong and resolute throughout twenty-seven years of prison. His fight against the injustice of apartheid led him to become the first South African president chosen in a truly representative and democratic election, and it helped him to find the compassion and forgiveness necessary for reconciliation and moving forward. Without purpose, Mandela could have become bitter and disillusioned. A purpose is too good a thing to waste.

You don't need to spend another day living without a purpose. What do you care about? What makes this day special? Remember, your purpose does not have to change the entire world to be worthwhile and give meaning to your day. Purpose is often found in the little things, such as watering plants or creating a garden, which brings life into the world. Purpose is fulfilled when we share our talents and gifts and in the kindnesses we show our family and friends, such as preparing a meal, giving an encouraging word, or listening with compassion and full presence. Purpose can also be about expressing our dearest values on a daily basis. Honesty, generosity, sexual responsibility, integrity, effort, compassion, wisdom, patience, and love are among the values we can bring to the world today through our actions. You might want to ask yourself regularly, *Is how I am acting today consistent with my deepest values?* Become more aware of how you express your values, and observe how living congruently makes you feel. When your energy is low or you feel drained, you may not be following your inner compass. Living our values boosts our energy and spirit.

No one else can determine your purpose for you. You are a unique being with unique purpose and potential. Finding your purpose is in itself a purpose. Here is an exercise to raise our awareness of purpose and how we manifest it.

Before leaving your home in the morning, write down one small and realistic purpose you want to achieve. This can be something as practical as survival, "earning a living so I can stay fed and keep a roof over my head." Or your purpose can tie into an altruistic value, such as bringing laughter or generosity into the world. Remember, a purpose doesn't have to change the entire world in a day to make a difference.

Notes

Epigraph. Phil Cousineau, *Once and Future Myths* (Boston: Conari Press, 2001), p. xx.

1.   Ralph Waldo Emerson, "Fortune of the Republic," *The Later Lectures of Ralph Waldo Emerson, 1843–1871, Volume 2: 1855–1871*, ed. Ronald A. Bosco and Joel Myerson (Athens, GA: University of Georgia Press, 2001), p. 321.

29. Open to the Heart of Simplicity

A tiny key unlocks an enormous door. A one-inch nail joins together measurements infinitely greater than itself.... Contentment with being small amid the great things of this world. This is the big-and-little known secret.

— DANIEL SKACH-MILLS

WHEN IS MORE REALLY LESS? I remember the time I met a project manager for a company that designs and manufactures flat-screen TVs. I was curious about how many "picture in picture" images were available at the time. He reported that the company's latest models could simultaneously display twelve different channels on one screen. "But we're working on displaying fifteen channels," he said proudly.

"Can people really use that many different images at once?" I wondered.

"No," he replied. "But more sells," he added with brightening eyes.

We are surrounded by an abundance of technology and goods. The standard supermarket carries upward of thirty thousand items. Surely the bounty before us is a blessing, and yet we also need to ask, At what cost?

The Amish have faced the struggle of keeping pace with their neighbors despite their limited use of technology in farming, which is still the mainstay of their lifestyle. They decided not to eliminate technology but to consciously accept into their lives only as much technology as they believe will not harm their community. Amish farmer Brad Igou writes in his book, *The Amish*: "We see our high-tech neighbor with the latest equipment, farming more acres quicker and getting higher yields and production than ever . . . going deeper and deeper into a spiral of debts that eventually bankrupt him. How is it then that the plain people [the Amish] have been able not only to continue farming but to actually expand their total acreage (often on smaller and smaller farms)?"[1]

Technology by itself is neither innately good nor bad. It provides many incredible benefits. It's how we decide to use technology and the boundaries we place around it that make the difference. While the Amish reduce technology in order to sustain a tight-knit community, there are other good reasons for experimenting with simplicity: for one, having less gives us less to worry about. How much do we really need to feel content? What are the simple things that give joy and fulfillment?

Robert Biswas-Diener has been called "the Indiana Jones of happiness" for his research on what makes people happy in different cultures around the world. In an interview, he told me the story of Manoj, a thirty-six-year-old rickshaw driver and father of three who lives in an illegal settlement at the southern end of Calcutta, India. As you might imagine, Manoj has an unimaginably stressful life. His family's home is made from bamboo covered with palm fronds and newspapers for walls. In this one-room shanty with a dirt floor, Manoj's wife cooks on a single kerosene stovetop. They have no running water, no electricity, and no heat, although plenty of mosquitoes. Manoj must walk one hour to reach his rickshaw, which he rents from its owner for half of what Manoj earns in a day, usually between two and three dollars. When Biswas-Diener asked Manoj what gives his life meaning, he answered, "I get up before sunrise, and my boys walk with me to the edge of the encampment. I like when they are there with me. And I like in the evening when they come home and ask me for toffee. I can't afford this, but the very fact that they have this expectation of me, that I could buy this, keeps me going."[2] Biswas-Diener's studies of Calcutta's slum-dwelling families actually show that they rated themselves with the same level of life satisfaction as U.S. college students typically reported.

A collective reevaluation, a process of realigning and redesigning the social system, is taking place in the United States and other parts of the world. These changes are as profound as the industrial and advertising revolutions, which spawned our present lifestyle. Today's questions pose new directions: How do we bring compassionate intelligence and simplicity to our choices? How can the planet support us unless we act as its steward in return? How do we act wisely knowing that every choice we make sends ripples of impact around the globe, touching people, communities, and other sentient life with whom we are unavoidably intertwined?

One way to invite compassionate intelligence and simplicity is to become conscious about the little choices we make each day. When he lived at Walden Pond, Henry David Thoreau penned this advice: "I say, let your affairs be as two or three, and not a hundred or a thousand; instead of a million, count half a dozen, and keep your accounts on your thumb nail.... Simplify, simplify. Instead of three meals a day, if it be necessary, eat but one; instead of a hundred dishes, five; and reduce other things in proportion."[3] This advice leads to more questions than answers because there is not one path to simplicity for everyone to follow. And as we find our own way, it is important not to become righteous, dogmatic, and judgmental. Try the following strategy to cultivate simplicity one moment at a time.

Embrace an attitude of simplicity. Begin by noting the simple pleasures that bring *enjoyment without using* unnecessary resources or energy. Examples of this include taking a walk, playing with a pet, being with family, looking at the stars or the moon, playing an instrument, reading a book, mindfully eating, or sharing a conversation. Also, reflect on what it would be like to live simply and peacefully in community.

Notes

Epigraph. Daniel Skach-Mills, *The Tao of Now* (Portland, OR: KenArnold Books, 2008), p. 79.

1. Brad Igou, *The Amish: In Their Own Words* (Scottdale, PA: Herald Press, 1999), p. 122.

2. Robert Biswas-Diener in an interview with the author, Portland, Oregon, December 21, 2007.

3. Henry David Thoreau, *Walden, Or Life in the Woods* (Charleston, SC: Forgotten Books, 2008), pp. 63–64.

30. Embrace Your Hero's Journey

*The big question is whether you are going to be able to say
a hearty yes to your adventure.*

— JOSEPH CAMPBELL

*J*OSEPH CAMPBELL SPENT A LIFETIME exploring the mythology of the hero as described in literature, art, and cultures throughout the world. "The hero's journey," as he called it, signifies the transformative journey we all travel when we face any major life transition or challenge. Our journey is not only physical but also an adventure amid the challenges of our mind, heart, and spirit. Typically, the mythical hero acquires something, maybe a sword or an elixir, that saves the day when things look most bleak. In *Star Wars*, for example, Luke Skywalker had a light saber and the force at his disposal. In our own stories, we can make use of mindfulness and Intentionally Centering Attention Now to confront what is unknown and unpleasant. We may not be able to choose the journey, but with mindfulness, we can choose to respond with full presence, respect, and dignity.

A stiff wind blows down the Hudson River on this unseasonably chilly spring day, as I approach a single-story home in upstate New York. Robert Mawson, a compact and distinguished-looking man with a British accent and a thick mane of wavy white hair, greets me and welcomes me inside. He has the distinction of being the only person to teach meditation at the United Nations. Robert is a picture of health, though he has had several close brushes with death. We sit down in his living room, which is filled with sacred objects from his various travels in Southeast Asia and other parts of the world. I notice among them pictures of his ordination as a monk in a Thai temple, as well as a large crystal ball sitting regally atop an ornately carved wooden stand.

Bob's life story resembles something out of a Charles Dickens novel. Born near Newcastle in England in 1943, he grew up in a coal mining community in an impoverished family of six children. Bob tells me he missed a lot of school because he was blind in his left eye. "I had very little education," he recalls, "and the options were to work on a farm or in a coal mine. However, I read in a boy's comic that you could join the British army as a junior leader; that when you turned eighteen, you could join the man's unit; and that the boys who trained this way became the senior noncommissioned officers and warrant officers of the future. I wanted that. But everyone, including my father, told me that you need two good eyes to join the army. I was fourteen years old, and I started to cry when I heard I couldn't join. Because I could see partially in my bad eye, I was sent to a civilian eye doctor to get glasses. When the doctor told me he couldn't correct my vision, I began to cry again. He gave me a pair of glasses then, which were made from ordinary glass, and a note. So, I got in."¹ Bob's dream of leaving his mining town was realized.

After twelve years of service, two leaking heart valves, aorta and mitral valves, were discovered in Bob. "I was born with them," he explains. "I left the army and went to live in Denmark. I was medically discharged. By the time I turned thirty-two, my heart was so weakened I needed two mechanical valves put in." In those days, patients with heart valves were told to be sedentary, but the sedentary lifestyle was definitely not for Bob. "I was a noncompliant patient. I went climbing mountains in Iran, Syria, Iraq, and the jungles of Thailand, Cambodia, and Laos. I also went to Greenland and Iceland and climbed mountains in America. I did all kinds of things the doctors thought were amazing. I kept on living. But I also had several cardiac arrests and was defibrillated back to life at least five times — twice by the same nurse in two different years. That nurse said to me, "Mr. Mawson, please don't come back to the ER when I'm on duty because you scare the hell out of me!"

In 1998, Bob had a defibrillator planted in his chest. The same year, he suffered double pneumonia twice and almost died. In 2002, he was told to prepare himself for a transplant and the heart of a twenty-three-year-old woman. Bob, who teaches meditation and disease prevention to healthcare workers, always understood that his mental outlook and ability to be mindful were critical to his survival. "I thought if I passed away, too many people would be sad, including me. I felt I'd already made an impact on many people's lives, but I wanted to continue," Bob recalls. "My hope was to survive and to continue to teach people to meditate so they could find inner peace and learn how to slow the aging process through good nutrition and lifestyle habits."

As he prepared for his transplant operation, Bob wanted to remain aware and mindful, even during surgery, so that he could positively influence and assist his body's healing. This was so important to him that he carried something with him on the stretcher the morning he was rolled to surgery. "When I went in for the heart operation," explains Bob, "I was listening to my meditation CD, and I had a smile on my face and a heart full of hope for my new heart and the success of the operation. What I knew from experience was that if my mind was calm and I used meditation, I could lower my blood pressure, and even under anesthesia, my unconscious mind would be meditating. Many people who go in for operations are afraid. Patients who are afraid bleed more than people who are not, and they don't heal quite as quickly, either."

Can you imagine being wheeled into a heart transplant operation with a smile on your face? That day Bob Mawson cheerfully greeted his surgeon, the well-known Dr. Mehmet Oz. "I asked Dr. Oz if I could listen to my CD the whole time they operated, and he said yes." Years after his transplant, Bob continues to do the work of making a difference in people's lives. "I think now that I meditate," affirms Bob, "I see things in people that often they don't see in themselves. I always look for the good in everyone, and generally, that's what I find. It's rather like the law of attraction."

Before I leave his house, Bob invites me to share lunch, and over a hearty bowl of vegetable soup, we exchange stories of our experiences as monks and discuss the importance of hope. Bob tells me his transformative journey has taught him never to give up. He has postherpetic neuralgia, which comes from shingles, and a depressed immune system from the medications used to keep his body from rejecting his new heart. Nonetheless, Bob uses his mind to enjoin his body, creating an inner state of peace and harmony. "What I do is I talk to the pain with my mind. I tell the pain, *I know you think you're tough but I'm more powerful than you'll ever be. You might bring me down, but you'll never keep me down. And one day I'll wake up, and you'll be gone. I'm in control of you; you're not in control of me.* And I use a meditation to concentrate on the pain, let it go, and dissipate it." Bob is determined to stay present with all aspects of his hero's journey, and he uses his story to inspire others.

If I have learned one thing from Bob, it is that mindfulness can be the elixir to help us say yes to letting go of the old and embracing what may come — whether that's a new job, undergoing therapy, starting treatment for addiction, going to college, facing an illness, or confronting divorce.

Like Bob Mawson, give yourself a reason for continuing on the journey, especially when the going gets tough. Also, put your journey in perspective: others have journeyed this same road and made it through. Seek out others whose journeys inspire you with hope and wisdom.

Notes

Epigraph. Joseph Campbell, *The Power of Myth*, with Bill Moyers (New York: Broadway, 1988), p. 161.

1.   All Robert Mawson quotations are from an interview with the author, Hastings-on-Hudson, New York, March 20, 2008.

True religion is real living; living with all one's soul,
with all one's goodness and righteousness.

— ALBERT EINSTEIN

SUPPOSE THERE ARE TWO HOUSES equally filled with riches. At one house, the windows are wide open and the door is left unlocked. At the other house, the windows and door are locked. In fact, this second house is also protected by an alarm system. Which house is going to be a target for thieves? Which is more likely to be robbed? A Tibetan meditation master used this analogy to make the point that if we don't want our most valuable treasures and assets to be stolen, we need the vigilant guards of ethics and mindfulness to stand watch. If we let down our guard, we might wake up to find that our house has been emptied and trashed.

I have been working with thirty-year-old Curtis for almost six months, helping him deal with social anxiety, which has impaired his ability to advance in his career. I have known about Curtis's dependence on alcohol to manage his anxiety, but although I have raised the issue before, he has never wanted to face it until today.

"I'm really sick and tired of waking up with hangovers," he tells me with a sense of desperation in his voice. "When I get home at night, all I want to do is get blitzed, and that's the only time I get to spend with my five-year-old daughter. I'm afraid that I'm doing the same thing my father did to me, and I just don't know if I can go on like this. I want to stop drinking. I've tried to quit many times over the years but haven't succeeded. I'm really disgusted and don't like where things are headed. What can I do?"

"This will require a lot of discipline, commitment, and a good plan," I tell him. Curtis and I talk about his willingness to change and what this will look like for him. Despite some fitful starts and stops, he eventually creates a plan to safeguard his most valuable treasure: his conscious awareness and presence to his family and future. His plan includes making an inventory of the triggers that lead him to drink, reducing stress with diaphragmatic breathing and exercise, and enlisting the help of his wife and others when necessary. Curtis experiences ups and downs on this journey, but I'm continually impressed by his courage and his resolve to move forward and stay present.

Ethics can be defined as a heart-centered approach to identifying and expressing basic goodness. Just as athletes train to improve their physical performance, ethics can be approached as a training for the heart and heart-based living. With regular practice, it becomes easier to recognize goodness and to avoid harm. A practical outcome of heart-centered living is that it makes life easier. It reduces the worry and suffering that come from causing harm. When we harm another, we must live not only with that inhumane transgression but also with the worry about being caught and all of the ramifications and the estrangement from family and friends that crime creates. It's highly unlikely, however, that you will end up doing jail time or suffer for heart-centered living.

Here are five trainings for the heart, known as the Five Precepts in Buddhism. You may well recognize these principles even if you've never heard of the Five Precepts. You do not need to limit yourself to these five and can consider them a starting point. The first teaching stipulates, *Do not harm any living beings.* The flip side of this teaching asks us to embrace and support all beings with loving-kindness. Empower them when you can, encourage, understand, and cherish them. This training asks us to look at our local and global situations and to recognize how our personal choices cause ripples that affect others. While the idea of not taking another's life is specific, the notion of loving-kindness for all beings is wide and inclusive. It's actually a more challenging instruction because it asks more of us. Don't let the enormity and significance of this first precept overwhelm you. A single drop more of kindness, love, and compassion to every being you meet today, including yourself, makes a difference.

The second training of the heart states, *Do not take what is not given or offered.* So, we do not steal, and we do not assume something is offered when it may not be. From another angle, this teaching is asking us to embrace generosity — and bear in mind that there are many forms of generosity we can extend. With mindfulness, we can be aware of how willing we are to give, emotionally and physically, to others.

The third training of the heart says, *Do not lie or speak falsely*. Some interpret this teaching to include not speaking with ill intent. The positive side of this instruction asks us to embrace truthfulness, which creates a trusting environment, free from gossip. You know that saying, "You're only as good as your word"? Well, mindful speech goes even further by alerting us not only to what we say but also to how we say it. We might also ask ourselves: *Would I say what I'm saying about this person if that person were included in this conversation?*

The fourth training advises, *Do not commit any sexual misconduct*. This is about not using our sexuality in a way that harms others. Sexual misconduct, of course, is only one way to abuse a relationship. This training encourages us to become more aware generally of harmful relationship behaviors and to make new choices accordingly. The flip side of this training speaks to how we embrace joy, contentment, trust, and openness in our relationships.

The last training of the heart advises, *Do not take any intoxicants or substances that can affect your awareness and mindfulness*. This is an important guard to have at our door; it requires an ongoing practice of Intentionally Centering Attention Now, which includes the awareness that we should nurture ourselves with wholesome foods and activities. This training also asks us to become more aware of how various forms of entertainment affect our consciousness. Notice if you are becoming numb or addicted because of a form of entertainment such as the Internet, and if you are, do something about it.

Take these trainings to heart, but also recognize that we are human and subject to frailty. You don't have to judge your behavior on an absolute scale. If you should happen to act out of greed, anger, lust, or violence, accept the truth of your action, experience the regret, and renew your commitment to practice the trainings with greater awareness. Remember that blame and shame are not trainings of the heart — but loving-kindness and forgiveness are. Here is one more strategy for heart-centered living.

Keep track of your heart trainings daily. For example, you can write the name of each training on a piece of paper and tape each to a different cup. Each night before going to bed, reflect on how you practiced a given training that day. Mark each of your efforts by putting a penny in the appropriate cup. At the end of the week, count the pennies in each cup to see which trainings need more attention. Don't be judgmental about the final tally. Give yourself credit for putting in the effort and making a commitment to heart-centered living.

Note

Epigraph. Linda Picone, ed., *The Daily Book of Positive Quotations* (Minneapolis: Fairview Press, 2008), p. 142.

32. Practice Silence

In the attitude of silence, the soul finds the path in a clearer light,
and what is elusive and deceptive resolves itself into crystal clearness.

— MOHANDAS GANDHI

HERE IS A POWER AND A KNOWING that flow from silence. Psychiatrist Elisabeth Kübler-Ross, a pioneer in
the field of death and dying, believed that the deep peace pro-
vided by silence can be found anywhere: "There is no need to
go to India or anywhere else to find peace. You will find that
deep place of silence right in your room, your garden, or even
your bathtub."[1] And Mother Teresa said of the connection
between silence and the divine: "We need to find God, and
He cannot be found in noise and restlessness. God is a friend
of silence."[2] In a world that is loud with commotion and clat-
ter, nothing may be more important than turning down the volume in order to open to the mystery, which is manifesting all
around.

A strong wind howls through the trees when I step out this evening. My mind wants to name the sound, to compare it to the sounds of a rainstorm or a faraway train, but I take a breath and try instead just to listen to what is. The warm wind brushes my face and chest, and now my mind wants to define the feeling — comfortable, similar to the breeze I remember from last week. I sit down on the grass, watching as the stars twinkle and the brightness of the moon casts long shadows from hundred-foot-high fir trees. The treetops sway in the wind. The moon's light is cool and soothing. I take another breath. Then another. And another.

It takes time to let the noises, images, and desires of a day — indeed, of a lifetime — fade away. They don't always. But for brief moments, it appears: silence. Just silence, just opening, just here. A glimpse. A gap. But the moment my mind grabs at the silence, it vanishes. I take another breath. I let go as I exhale, to let the silence in. Again. I listen to the silence of the mind. Strange thing, this silence. It contains so much beyond word, thought, and space. Frogs, crickets, buzzing insects, all join with the wind to compose this song of silence. Soon, this song fades too, and sounds return. The volume is turned back up, and I am sitting in the backyard once again, listening to the howling wind.

No one will give you silence, but if you're not careful, it can be stolen from you. I am reminded of Sammy, a teenage boy. In our first session, Sammy goes into extreme detail telling me about the video games he spends hours playing. When I comment on his extraordinary recall of the games, he says, "They really help my imagination." At some point, I ask him if he has ever thought of creating worlds of his own, without any help from his games.

"I tried, but I always get headaches."

"Do you only get them when you try to imagine things?" I ask.

"No, I also get them whenever there's a lot of noise," he replies.

"But aren't your video games loud?"

"Yeah, they're really loud, but they don't give me headaches."

Like many of us, Sammy finds it upsetting to have silence in his life — a growing challenge in our overstimulating environment.

Have you heard the tale about a journalist who travels to Africa to interview a tribal chief? He is told he must first sit in silence with the chief before speaking with him. When the journalist asks why, he is told that it is the traditional way tribal members become acquainted with others. After sitting with the chief in silence, the journalist will be permitted to ask as many questions as he wants, so the journalist agrees. He sits opposite the chief, and they just look into each other's eyes. After a few uncomfortable minutes, the journalist waits for a signal that the silent introduction is over. But none is given. Ten more minutes pass, then twenty, then thirty, then sixty. According to the story, they sit in silence for two hours. When the chief signals that the introduction is over and the journalist is informed he can ask his questions, he respectfully bows and says that he has none. He discovered that what he received from this intimate silent communication was richer than anything he might gather from words alone.

I have experienced this myself and led others in this form of silent communication. After getting past the giggles and initial discomfort of looking into the eyes of someone you don't know, a deep sense of trust, knowing, understanding, and connection arises that words cannot convey. Trappist monk Thomas Merton addressed the role of silence in relationship when he wrote, "It is in deep solitude that I find the gentleness with which I can truly love my brothers. . . . Solitude and silence teach me to love my brothers for what they are, not for what they say."[3]

Silence is a special gift that comes wrapped in many shapes. How you invite silence into your life will be as unique as you are. Here is one way to begin.

Unplug yourself. Devote time each day to turning down the volume on electronic devices in order to be present with what is. Let yourself sit for a few minutes with no agenda. Listen for the silence that is present between your thoughts. Let your mind take a rest and be blessed in its true nature.

Notes

Epigraph. Richard Leider and David Shapiro, *Repacking Your Bags: Lighten Your Load for the Rest of Your Life* (San Francisco: Berrett-Koehler, 2002), p. 40.

1. Lama Surya Das, *Awakening to the Sacred: Creating a Spiritual Life from Scratch* (Broadway: New York, 1999), p. 362.
2. Mother Teresa, *The Joy in Loving: A Guide to Daily Living* (New York: Penguin, 2000), p. 403.
3. Thomas Merton, *The Sign of Jonas* (New York: Harvest Books, 2002), p. 268.

33. Mind Your Spirit

*Those who dwell among the beauties and mysteries of the earth
are never alone or weary of life.*

— RACHEL CARSON

PRACTICING MINDFULNESS DOES NOT MEAN that we won't
still find ourselves overcome with doubt. There will be
periods when purpose is hard to find, when the journey seems
like a chore, and when you're not sure if your values and
choices are making a difference. The truth is, we just don't
know. Now that we have arrived at this place, where is it? You
might think of this as the intersection where *don't know, mystery, emptiness,* and *doubting mind* meet. It's a good sign that
you have finally arrived here in present time. How wonderful!
But wait a moment, you may be thinking. *You say I'm in this
place and it's wonderful, but I feel lost.* Being lost is greatly underrated. It can mean that you are in a place of unknowing where the rational mind cannot go. In the way that we
need darkness to see the stars, we similarly need unknowing to

become a beginner again and engage with the mystery and wonder of it all.

There were once two scholars, both well known and respected, who worked in the same academic field. One of the scholars, Benjamin, had just written a new book and was giving a talk in the city where the second scholar lived. The second scholar, Martin, came to listen and was impressed with what he heard. Afterward, Martin introduced himself to Benjamin.

"Would you be interested in sharing some ideas? If so, it would be my pleasure to invite you to my home for tea."

"I love exploring new ideas," replied Benjamin. "Let me pack up my things and we can go."

When they arrived at Martin's house, tea was prepared and the two began conversing. But each time Martin brought up an idea to explore, Benjamin went on to talk only about his book and his research. Hardly pausing for a breath, Benjamin laid out the reasons for his theories. This continued for an hour, even though Martin tried to engage Benjamin in dialogue.

During Benjamin's monologue, Martin noticed that his guest's teacup was empty and asked, "Would you like more tea?" Benjamin nodded, as he spoke about the validity of his studies. Martin slowly lifted the pot of tea and poured until the tea reached the top edge of the cup. Benjamin glanced at this but kept talking. Then Martin tilted the pot and continued to pour tea as it overflowed Benjamin's cup. With tea streaming over the saucer and onto the table, the talkative Benjamin finally stopped.

"What are you doing?" he asked, shocked. "Can't you see that you've poured more into that cup than it will hold?"

"You said you wanted to explore and share ideas, but you are like this cup of tea," Martin answered, "too full of your own ideas to have space for anything else."

It is okay — in fact, it is quite *one-derful* — to be in a state of unknowing. It is an opportunity to practice beginner's mind, a place of nonclinging, nonattachment, and nonidentification. Here, your cup doesn't overflow, and unlimited space is available. Whenever the cup fills up and overflows with I-me-my-mine, you can empty the cup with awareness and then rest in the wonderment and mystery of that. The more you empty your cup, the more you may know and dwell in the beauty that is simply here. Just here. Just vast and open. Like the sky.

Review all the spirit key teachings. Identify one that you feel will enrich your life and deepen your understanding at this time. Vow to engage in your chosen practice every day for the next week. At the end of the week, write down the changes you notice in yourself. In what ways have you become more aware? Select another spirit key teaching to practice the next week.

Note

Epigraph. *Dwelling: Webster's Quotations, Facts and Phrases* (San Diego, CA: ICON Group International, 2008), p. 1.

PART FOUR

THE RELATIONSHIP KEY

*N*O MEMBER OF OUR HUMAN GLOBAL COMMUNITY is whole until all members are cared for and well. For that reason, we need to regain a sense of mutual trust and hope if we are to thrive together. The relationship key unlocks the many benefits of connecting with others. Breaking through confusion and finding support and resources come naturally once you start using the keys of cooperation, deep listening, presence, compassion, and loving-kindness.

34. Give Others Your Full Presence

Some people feel more alive when they travel and visit unfamiliar places or foreign countries because at those times sense perception — experiencing — takes up more of their consciousness than thinking. They become more present.

— ECKHART TOLLE

*P*ERHAPS YOU HAVE HEARD THE STORY of the man who went to a mind-training center that promised enlightenment — total presence, clarity of mind, and enduring sense of peace — all in just a single day. When he inquired what he needed to do in order to attain this liberated state of being, the teacher told him he needed only to follow his breath completely for seven straight hours. "Notice and be fully present with your inbreath, your outbreath, and the pause between your breaths, and you will attain your enlightenment," said the teacher while handing the man a meditation cushion. *This is excellent*, thought the man as he glanced at his watch. *I can have my enlightenment by the time I get home for dinner!*

Excited, the fellow sat on his cushion and immediately started following his breath. It went really well for the first breath, but then a car honked loudly outside the center. His sense of hearing grabbed onto the sound of the horn and brought it into his mind. *How rude to honk like that*, he thought to himself. *Don't people realize we're in here trying to get our enlightenment?* And then he realized that he had forgotten all about his breath, and so, he immediately returned his attention to the breath. All went well for two whole breaths, until a fly buzzed nearby. The man opened his eyes and saw the fly circling about, and what he saw led him to think, *I bet someone left the window open. I ought to tell someone about this. Who's in charge here?* And suddenly, he realized that he had lost track of his breath again. He returned to observing the breath. As the story goes, the man was still there ten years later, trying to be present with his breath for seven consecutive hours. Why is it so difficult to train our minds to stay present with each fresh moment as it arises? It seems as if this would be an easy thing to do.

My former monk "brother" U Thitzana has traveled from his monastery in Los Angeles to stay at my home in Portland for a few days. A traditional Theravada monk since the age of twelve, when he was ordained in Burma, U Thitzana is atypical because he is a scholar widely versed in all religions. I look forward to our conversations about spiritual topics. One night I introduce him to my own meditation group, where he gives a talk and leads us in meditation. Another night I drive him to the other side of town, where again he teaches. On two evenings, after I return home from my work at an intensive psychiatric outpatient clinic, a small but telling interaction with U Thitzana teaches me an important lesson.

Fatigued after the long day at the clinic, I stop by the mail-box and pick up a stack of mail before trudging into the house. All is quiet, and in a rote manner, I sit down at the dining room table and start sorting through the mail. In a few moments, as if out of nowhere, my friend appears at my side.

"Hello, Donald!" he cheerfully intones, greeting me with a broad and welcoming smile. His saffron-colored robe hangs loosely over his thin frame.

"Hi, Thitzana. It's good to see you," I answer with as much energy as I can muster while prying open another envelope. "How was your day?" I ask, not realizing that I am actually paying more attention to the letter than to my friend.

"I can see that you're busy now. I'll come back later," he says kindly, without any hint of negative emotion. He retreats to his room so quietly that when I look up I'm surprised to find he is already walking away.

"I'll be with you shortly," I say, all the while continuing with my mail.

I finish as quickly as I can before going to Thitzana's room. The door is open, and I find him reading. He puts down his book and joins me in the living room for some hot tea. I discover that he has spent the day reading, meditating, and walking around the grounds of the house. Later that night we sit together in meditation. The open windows draw in a cool evening breeze and the song of a tree frog with its backup band of crickets.

Early the next morning, before I get ready to leave for the clinic, U Thitzana has already made his own breakfast and washed the dishes. Contentedly and quietly, he sits upright in a chair reading another book. Although I have known him for some years, I find myself thinking, *He's like the perfect guest because you don't even know he is there.* I bid him a good day and make the nearly hour-long drive back to the clinic. That evening I return home, again exhausted with mail in hand. As though in a scene from the movie *Groundhog Day* — in which Bill Murray's character relives the same day, over and over — I sit down at the dining room table and begin opening the mail, and my friend suddenly appears before me, as if out of the mist.

"Hello, Donald, my friend!" he beams enthusiastically.

"Hi, Thitzana. It's good to see you too," I reply, my attention partially engrossed in mechanical letter opening.

"You're busy now. We can talk later," he says brightly, somehow managing to disappear by the time I raise my head to look at him. Only this time, something different happens. *Wake up!* growls a somewhat irritated inner voice. Suddenly, like a bolt between my eyes, it hits me. My friend does not want just a part of me but my complete being, my full attention. He is asking for one fundamental thing, I realize: my full presence. I set down the unopened mail, make my way back to Thitzana's room, and apologize. I often refer to this kind of wake-up call as "a mindfulness booster shot."

Everyone benefits when presence is developed. At a time when a riot of distractions vies for our attention, it's easy to forget that full presence is one of the most precious gifts we can offer one another. When you give others your full presence, you are more alive and alert. You may also find you gain the presence of others. Should you ever have the opportunity to have a monk visit with you, I heartily endorse it, but if that is not possible, try the strategy below to support your complete presence in the company of another.

Avoid distractions and multitasking when you talk with someone. Don't watch TV and converse at the same time, and avoid the phone, texting, and email when you are in someone else's company. If you urgently need to contact someone else, excuse yourself so you can contact that person with full attention!

Note

Epigraph. Eckhart Tolle, *A New Earth: Awakening to Your Life's Purpose* (New York: Penguin, 2008), p. 239.

35. Embrace Silence and Deep Listening

A late summer night and the snowy egret
has come again to the shallows in front of my house

as he has for forty years.
Don't think he is a casual part of my life,

that white stroke in the dark.

— MARY OLIVER, "SNOWY EGRET"

SOCIAL SITUATIONS OFTEN EVOKE ANXIETY as well as excitement. This is especially so when we are meeting new
people. How can we bridge that gap of awkwardness? How can
we begin to know someone better? Some people find it uncomfortable to allow silence into a conversation, while others
feel safe only when asking the questions or interacting superficially. And while a casual understanding may be perfectly okay
for certain relationships and acquaintances, what is lost when
we view the world and others superficially? There are ways to
move beyond shallow-speak and to break out of our individual
perspective. The doorway into another's world can be found
when we allow space for silence and deep listening. To venture
into and experience this space is to discover that each of us is
really the essence of pure meaning and attention.

From a picturesque house nestled on a bay minutes from the craggy coastline of Rhode Island, I witness a white egret lingering at the water's edge. Moments later, I raptly watch a rust-red fox and her two cubs play on a grassy field near the bay. I don't observe these events alone. I am joined by eight others. We have traveled here from around the country to spend a weekend working on behalf of a nonprofit organization. This is the first time the entire group has been together in person — other than talking on the telephone. For many of us, this is our first face-to-face meeting. Being here with everyone is energizing and affirming, and it makes what we are trying to accomplish feel more real, possible, and hopeful. Although there is a fair share of animated conversation, our work is punctuated by long periods of stillness. Now, in silence, we marvel at the nature just a stone's throw from the large picture window at the back of the house.

One of my favorite moments occurs on the second day. It is a sunny morning, not long after dawn, when I shuffle onto a creaky wooden dock overlooking the bay. Two others already sit in silent meditation, and as I slowly seat myself cross-legged on a cushion, I feel as if I am a link being added to an unbroken chain. I feel the sun flickering on my eyelids and inhale the fresh sea breeze with each slow breath. After about half an hour, I open my eyes and find that others have joined us on the dock.

Back in the house, I silently prepare a simple breakfast. I take a cup of yogurt, a scoop of granola, and a slice of bread with butter on top. I eat, savoring all the flavors, and enjoy a cup of strong coffee someone has already brewed. By eight o'clock, everyone is ready to discuss plans for the coming year. We talk about the group's purpose and connect the dots in what is still a relatively young organization. All the while, it seems we never really forget about the beauty of the bay. Frequently, we take a one-to-five-minute break in the middle of discussions to sit in silence, mindfully breathe, reflect, or look outside at nature's splendor. These moments to pause and contemplate always seem to help the group get centered and back on track when we become stuck or unsure about the direction to move in next. I cannot help but wonder how many other relationships — among colleagues, friends, and family, for example — would benefit from a mindful or meditative break. Silence prepares us for listening and opening to others.

Our nonprofit group also makes time to go outside to enjoy lunch on the sunny deck, to stroll the quiet neighborhood, and to walk a narrow footpath that skirts the bay. One afternoon we drive the van to the ocean and enjoy a long walk along the beach. This gives me time to get to know better those whom I have largely spoken with via conference calls. We enjoy one-on-one conversations as bubbly waves curl up near our feet and then recede into the ocean's edge. There is quiet between the words, space to thoughtfully soak in ideas, feel the wet sand beneath our feet, and ask a clarifying question or two. We are new friends learning about one another. Our conversations and the pockets of mindfulness during this ocean walk encourage and sustain our group. I cannot help but feel a sense of hope, joy, and optimism.

George Washington Carver, the botanist and educator who discovered hundreds of uses for the peanut and the sweet potato, routinely awakened before dawn to sit in the stillness with his plants. He listened intently to the darkness outside for secrets that he knew the crops would share. "Anything will give up its secrets if you love it enough," Carver explained. "Not only have I found that when I talk to the little flower or to the little peanut they will give up their secrets, but I have found that when I silently commune with people they give up their secrets also — if you love them enough."[1]

Don't be afraid to make space for the silence and stillness when you are with others. By listening to others with your full attention and presence, you offer a gift that is not often tendered in this day and age. A good strategy for deepening friendships is loving, compassionate, open, and kind listening.

Let yourself listen to another with a warm, tender heart. Look within and see if you can open with kindness to another's point of view. Instead of jumping in with your opinions and judgments, try reflecting back what you have just heard, without interpreting or judging it. After sharing, you can ask, "Is that what you meant?" Active listening takes time to learn, so be patient.

Notes

Epigraph. "Snowy Egret," from *Evidence* by Mary Oliver (p. 10), copyright © 2009 by Mary Oliver. Reprinted by permission of Beacon Press, Boston.

1.   Wendell P. Loveless, *Manual of Gospel Broadcasting* (Whitefish, MT: Kessinger, 2005), p. 154.

36. Share Loving-Kindness with Others

No lesson is learned well until you share it with others — joyfully.

— FRANK COPPIETERS

*I*N CHAPTER 24, you learned the first part of an ancient meditation for receiving love and the gifts of others. Now it is time for the second part of this practice, which is to give love to your teachers, family, friends, and others. It is no accident that the complementary polarities of receiving and giving are at the core of loving-kindness meditation. When we accept and offer loving-kindness with an open heart, we can also overcome our fears and limitations. This practice teaches us that to judge giving or receiving in terms of strength and weakness is a mistake. Receiving and giving are two sides of one key that heals.

It is a Saturday morning, a couple of days into the new year, when I get in my car and head out to the Portland Rescue Mission. My wife and I are donating sweaters, shirts, an electric blanket, and other needed items during a period of unusually cold weather. On the way, I stop at the post office to mail some packages. While we are waiting in line, the man in front of me strikes up a conversation. With a slight drawl in his words, he asks if I have seen any of the college football bowl games.

"No, not really," I answer. I almost never watch college football. There is a hint of disappointment, almost sadness, in his face. It's obvious that he wants to connect with someone on this subject. "Well, actually, I heard about that Alabama game," I say, recalling the replays that were on the news. He brightens and in moments is talking about his favorite team, the Texas Longhorns. I don't know anything about the Longhorns, and I learn from this fellow that their university has a well-respected health sciences department. Our conversation is cut short, however, when the lone postal clerk calls out, "Next." The Longhorns fan steps off to the side to fill out some forms, and I take care of my business at the counter. Upon leaving, I notice that he is stuffing individual bags of fresh ground coffee into a flat-rate box.

"That's going to make someone very happy," I say, displaying my liking for good coffee.

"Here, take one. You'll like it," he says without hesitation, holding out one of the silver-colored bags.

"Are you sure?" I ask, my hand already on the exit door handle.

"Yes," he answers, smiling.

"Thank you. That's very kind of you," I say, accepting the bag and feeling warmed inside by this gentle, spontaneous act of loving-kindness. There was a time when I wouldn't have taken this gift. My experience in the monastery, though, helped me understand the importance of accepting a gift given willingly.

A short drive later, I arrive at the Portland Rescue Mission. Two women accept our donation with broad smiles. "We really need this," one of them comments. I nod, heartened by the thought that someone will be a little warmer this winter season. And I will enjoy the gift of fresh, hot coffee when I get home.

By now, you have become familiar with part one of the loving-kindness blessing. Here you will begin as before, starting with forgiveness and then sending the following blessing of loving-kindness to yourself.

> *May I be safe,*
> *May I be happy,*
> *May I be healthy,*
> *May I be at peace.*
>
> *May I be free from pain,*
> *May I be free from hunger,*
> *May I be free from all suffering.*

When you open yourself to receive this blessing, you may notice a pleasant feeling — a warmth, a calmness, or simply a knowing. Take as much time as you need. If you have a difficult time accepting this blessing, picture yourself as a fully deserving young child or baby. If that doesn't help, think about someone or even something you have loved, such a child, a pet, or a teddy bear. Feel this love, and know that you can feel this love for yourself as well. Even if you don't yet believe the words, isn't it better to state a loving-kindness affirmation than to repeat, *I hate myself, I hate myself, I hate myself*?

Once you feel the blessing for yourself inwardly, you can start sending loving-kindness to others in the following order. Begin by sending the blessing to your teachers and guides, then to family members, followed by friends, people for whom your feelings are neutral, unfriendly people, and finally all beings. Either use individuals' names or say "my teachers, my family, my friends" when you want to bless these individuals as a group. Neutral people are those you encounter but don't really know, such as the cashier at a store and others whom you similarly see from time to time but have no real knowledge about. Unfriendly people are those you may not like or those who have actually done you harm. When you extend this blessing to all beings, you can begin by sending out the loving-kindness blessing to your neighborhood, then include all beings in your city, state, and country, all countries, all sentient beings on the planet, all planets, all solar systems, all galaxies, and all universes. "All beings" means not just humans but all living beings, whatever their level of sentience.

May _____ be safe.
May _____ be happy.
May _____ be healthy.
May _____ be at peace.

May _____ be free from pain.
May _____ be free from hunger.
May _____ be free from all suffering.

While you are offering the blessing, visually picture the recipient looking radiant and happy. You can repeat your blessing for anyone for as long as you want. If at any time you feel as though your storehouse of loving-kindness has been depleted, send loving-kindness to yourself again. Keep replenishing loving-kindness as needed. Once you feel replenished, again send loving-kindness blessings to others. When you have completed the loving-kindness meditation, you can conclude with these final words:

> *May suffering ones be suffering free,*
> *May the fearstruck fearless be,*
> *May grieving ones shed all grief,*
> *May all beings find relief.*

Here are two gentle ways to practice loving-kindness:

Have a conversation with someone you normally don't talk with. Give them your understanding and compassion. This might be that person at the drive-through window.

Another practice is to try to have loving-kindness and compassion for someone you don't understand or someone who pushes your buttons. The purpose is not to let yourself be abused but to learn to love in a more spacious and less conditional way.

Note

Epigraph. Frank Coppieters, *Handbook for the Evolving Heart* (Marina del Rey, CA: Conflu:x Press, 2006), p. 53.

37. Be Genuine and Real

You can play a shoestring if you're sincere.

— JOHN COLTRANE

THERE IS A STORY OF HOW THE BUDDHA once gave a talk to hundreds of monks, only to have them disagree and walk out on him. Did the Buddha then try to spin his message to get high approval ratings and win the monks over? No — he stood by his teaching rather than trying to make his talk more agreeable to his audience. Did he take the monks' response personally? If he had, the conflict could have driven the monks away for good. The Buddha instead trusted that if the monks found his words valuable, they would return. And they did.

When we crave approval, we may never find our authentic voice or establish honest relationship. As Lao Tzu taught, "Care about people's approval and you will be their prisoner."[1] Trusting your feelings, though, does not mean bludgeoning another over the head with your version of truth. Being genuine is not about winning or losing.

If we want to be authentic with others, we need to be in contact with our emotions as well as our thoughts. Take a moment to sense your emotional state right now. You can do this by closing your eyes and looking within, beyond words or concepts. See if you can enter more consciously into the physical aspect of the self that breathes, aches, itches, tires, moves and throbs with sensation, and carries consciousness. Sense the character, quality, or tonality of what you find. You could experience this feeling in any number of ways — as lightness, pleasantness, relaxation, tightness, or pain, for example. Whatever the feeling is, how well do you trust it? Can you tune into your emotional state when you interact with others? The signals your body sends help you to be real as you develop meaningful and lasting relationships.

Brain science shows the importance of accessing the body's emotions and intuition. In his book *Descartes' Error*, neuroscientist Antonio Damasio describes how a patient who could not access emotion spent more than thirty minutes trying to choose between two appointment times. Using logic only, the patient's detailed analysis still did not lead to a decision. According to Damasio, we need the body's instincts when making decisions because its memories of wobbliness in the legs (fear), pleasantness in the gut (joy), or heaviness in the body (fatigue) reinforce what we feel in the present moment. The ability to access knowledge from the body — both in the moment and from the past — is especially helpful in situations requiring trust.

What if you don't trust that feeling or gut instinct? Such is the case with Teresa, a petite woman in her thirties with shoulder-length blonde hair and sad blue eyes. Though she is casually dressed in jeans, a loose-fitting white blouse, and a blue blazer when I first meet her, nothing else about her seems very casual or relaxed. Teresa is so distraught during our initial meeting that she can hardly speak through her tears. Her anxiety is palpable. The story that unfolds is of a woman who does not trust her reality or her emotions. With unpredictable, alcoholic parents, Teresa never felt safe enough to express her feelings at home. When she tried, her parents discounted her feelings. At eighteen, Teresa married a man who gave to her financially but not emotionally or sexually. For the next fifteen years, Teresa dutifully raised three children but continued to suppress her feelings and carry on as if everything were okay. She harbored a secret crush on a man she met through friends and finally had an affair with him. When her marriage broke up, Teresa was shattered because she felt she had betrayed her sacred role as a mother.

In fact, Teresa continually betrays herself because she does not trust her deep, inner feelings. Like Damasio's patient, Teresa depends on her intellect in her effort to improve her new relationship, but the result is that she is exhausted by the non-stop analysis of her guilt and of potential responses to her partner's actions. I also learn that Teresa is an avid meditator who believes that feelings are illusory and so are invalid. For her, meditation has become another way to avoid feelings. I explain to Teresa that mindfulness of the body helps us to make sense of our relationships, as well as creating balance between our thoughts and our emotions. The point is not to become overwhelmed by emotions. Although our emotions give us valuable information, dwelling on negative emotions, such as anger or jealousy, is unhealthy. Both thoughts and emotions are necessary for establishing center. This integration leads to a balance of information, healthier boundaries, and better decisions. This is how we get real with ourselves and others.

Eventually, Teresa starts listening to her body's feelings during those times when her partner is unresponsive, insensitive, or unwilling to share. Instead of ignoring her emotions and trying to use her mind to discount or rationalize them away, she starts to observe and value the signals her body sends. If it feels like a punch in the gut, then there has been a punch in the gut. If it feels like sadness, sadness is present. Eventually, Teresa begins to process her feelings and to share them with her partner. At first, she finds it difficult to tolerate her feelings as a means of becoming congruent and whole, but the result is that she becomes empowered in her relationship and begins to participate as an equal.

Try the following strategy for getting real and trusting your genuine self in relationship.

Pay attention to the feelings you experience in a relationship: joy, peace, calm, mistrust, fear, sadness, anger, hurt, tiredness, and so forth. Locate the feeling in your body. Accept each feeling as a signal that is telling you something about your relationship. Notice if you rationalize or push away the feeling. Show patience, loving-kindness, and compassion for yourself as you acquire the courage to be genuine about your feelings. Keep breathing and accepting your emotions as they arise. If this becomes too painful or too uncomfortable, you can always take a break by focusing your attention elsewhere — but don't ignore the wisdom of the body.

Notes

Epigraph. Diane Durston, *Wabi Sabi: The Art of Everyday Life* (North Adams, MA: Storey, 2006), p. 192.

1. Lao Tzu, *Tao Te Ching: A New English Version*, trans. Stephen Mitchell (New York: Harper Perennial, 2006), p. 9.

38. Seek Out Happy and Meaningful Connections

Take the time to declare a happy hunting ground in your house
and in your feelings, and hunt there every day.

— DON GERRARD

WE CAN LEARN A LOT FROM THE LOST BOYS OF SUDAN, as they are called. When their families and villages were massacred in raids during the horrific civil war that lasted more than twenty years, many boys escaped into the bush. At least 27,000 boys endured an epic survival journey of several hundred miles — suffering attack and starvation — until they made their way to Ethiopia. Their tragic ordeal, however, was not over. When the refugee camps in Ethiopia closed, they were forced to return to Sudan and another life-threatening trek to the safety of Kenya. Although they were refugees who had lost their families, these traumatized boys developed their own relationships and community in the refugee camp. They found ways to celebrate together and to support one another. Many who successfully transitioned to other countries brought with them the knowledge and experience of life-saving relationships that nurture us with joy and meaning.

Difficult life journeys profoundly affect our moods. What's more, our moods can shift many times during a given day. But when we place mindful attention on developing our relationships, we may discover, as did the Lost Boys of Sudan, that those relationships bring us happiness — even during those times when all seems lost.

In the past several years, science has found evidence to support the idea that happiness increases when we surround ourselves with happy people. For example, Nicholas Christakis, a Harvard Medical School professor, and James Fowler, a natural and social sciences professor with the University of California at San Diego, led a study that found that social networks act as a circuit through which happiness spreads. Researchers examined the relationships of more than five thousand individuals who were initially part of the 1948 Framingham Heart Study, which examined the causes of cardiovascular disease. A second generation of participants joined the study in 1971, giving researchers a social network that was expanded to several degrees of separation for each volunteer. The study shows that negative factors such as obesity and smoking tend to spread among networks — but so does a positive factor such as happiness.

Christakis writes, "We've found that your emotional state may depend on the emotional experiences of people you don't even know, who are two to three degrees removed from you."[1] According to the findings, knowing an individual who is happy produces a 15.3 percent greater likelihood that you will be happier as well — there's even a 9.8 percent increase in your chances of being happy if one of your friends has a happy friend.[2] I guess you could call it "two-degrees-of-separation happiness": proximity is a compelling aspect of happiness. Having a happy friend or relative who lives in another city will not significantly affect one's happiness, though, because happiness seems to thrive through contact. You catch it, much like a cold, only from physically close contact with others. Researchers also found that connecting with others via the Internet or telephone does not produce the same degree of happiness that occurs with face-to-face contact.

How can another's happiness (or sadness, anxiety, or depression) affect our mood state? One of the answers is found in the brain, specifically in mirror neurons, which are the brain cells that fire whenever you do something (such as waving your hand) or watch another do something (waving their hand). In fact, sticking out your tongue at an infant will cause the infant to do the same. Mirror neurons are implicated in the way we learn; they also have a relational and survival purpose by letting us know what others are feeling. When we see someone smile, the mirror neurons of smiling in our brain are activated as well. Brain scientists believe mirror neurons are one reason we can experience empathy. Have you ever felt the sadness or grief another is experiencing? This is a form of mindful inner sight. It is also an awareness we can cultivate.

When we seek out others for support, it is important to be selective — this is critical for those with a personal history of abusive or harmful relationships. (If this is the case, "Prime Your Mind for Trust," chapter 7, would be a helpful step too.) Look for people who are proactive and empathetic.

I can still vividly recall a time when I needed to find the right kind of support — and needed to find it right away. I had just begun my mental health internship at a large HMO. The head of the internship program, Greg, shared with us, in mythic journey terms, that our first days on the unit would be like "making a descent into a dark cave," from which he hoped we would recover. I did not take him too seriously at the time, but I should have. Those first days at the clinic, I saw patients with a range of acute clinical problems, from bipolar disorder to suicidal ideation, issues I had not expected to see so soon. When one of my patients, a sensitive eighteen-year-old woman, tried to commit suicide, I was devastated. After being contacted by the emergency triage department about her condition, I hung up the phone and stared helplessly out my window at the small courtyard, where I had seen her strolling after leaving my office less than a week earlier. I went outside to get some air, thoughts swirled in my head, and I was left wondering what I could have done differently. My kind and insightful supervisors, Kathy and John, were there to guide me through this and many other difficult situations, but as helpful as they were, I faced other concerns that demanded a different kind of support.

After my first day on the job, for example, I needed to stay late to finish charting and treatment plans. To add to my first-day confusion, I didn't have an office (none of the interns did), only a compact file cart on wheels, which I rolled to a different unused office each day. The computerized system seemed indecipherable, with different systems for email, charting, and appointments, and I couldn't figure out how to schedule appointments from my computer. I came home feeling overwhelmed, defeated, and totally drained. It was pitch-black outside when I climbed into the Jacuzzi and sat there as the jets hummed and the heat absorbed the tension from my body. For a few brief moments, I had the sinking feeling in my gut that maybe I wouldn't make it through my internship. In fact, I thought, *Maybe this is the wrong career for me. I've made a huge mistake. I've spent thousands of dollars and almost three years on something that isn't right for me.* I swallowed hard and felt my heart sink. It was a pivotal and defining moment. I needed to locate specialized, positive support. The next day, I sought out other interns to compare our experiences and exchange support. We were all feeling overwhelmed, so we planned a group dinner to share stories, let the steam out, and explore a fresh perspective. Coming together in this way was a healing experience. It was also an effective way to locate happiness, connecting to individuals in close proximity both physically and emotionally.

Here is one way to create joy and happiness in your social connections:

Share a joke or uplifting story with someone. Almost everyone is willing to listen when someone asks, "Did you hear the joke about . . . ?" Remember, we're all making the journey through this world together, so why not lighten it up?

Notes

Epigraph. Don Gerrard, *One Bowl: A Guide to Eating for Body and Spirit* (Cambridge, MA: DaCapo Press, 2001), p. 121.

1. Harvard Medical School Office of Public Affairs, "Happiness Is a Collective — Not Just Individual — Phenomenon," http://web.med .harvard.edu/sites/RELEASES/html/christakis_happiness.html (accessed June 2009).

2. Nicholas Christakis and James Fowler, "Happiness, Social Networks, and Health," Online British Medical Journal 337 (a2781), December 4, 2008, www.bmj.com/cgi/content/extract/337/dec04_2/a2781 (accessed June 2009).

39. Untie the Knots of Emotional Entanglement

The advantage of the emotions is that they lead us astray.

— OSCAR WILDE

HAVE YOUR EMOTIONS EVER LED YOU ASTRAY? Have they ever caused you to suffer? Have they ever left you feeling overwhelmed, confused, and unable to make good decisions? Human beings are emotional. Our brain is wired for emotion, and our body is wired to respond quickly to the cascade of hormones and chemicals that even a simple kiss produces. We need to respect this biological part of our makeup, yet how do we do so and at the same time untie the knots of negative emotions we experience?

Samantha is a tall, attractive woman in her midthirties. Her straight, silky black hair cascades over her shoulders, and she frequently brushes it away from her eyes and forehead. "My mother keeps bringing up my failures over and over," she says, frustrated.

"How do you respond to that?" I ask.

"I feel helpless. When I tell her that she repeats the same stories, she denies it. And if I get angry, she just hangs up on me."

"Then what happens?"

"I usually end up calling her back and just ignoring what happened before. It wouldn't do any good for me to bring it up again anyway; she'd just deny it ever happened."

I witnessed this relationship directly some months later when Samantha's mother came in for a family session. Samantha voiced her feelings about having her mother repeat a particularly hurtful story. Then an interesting thing happened: Samantha's mother denied ever doing this and then launched into the objectionable story right before my eyes! When I gently interrupted her and asked if she was aware that she was now telling the story, she looked at me as though I needed therapy. And yet, Samantha couldn't stay away from her mother. Like a moth to a flame, she kept returning to the fire, hoping that somehow the outcome would be different next time. Sadly, it never was.

The most influential relationships in our lives are those with family. How our family and caregivers relate to us at a very young age prepares us for future relationships. In these tender and vulnerable years, we discover how to communicate our needs. If our parents or caregivers are regularly frustrated, impatient, angry, unresponsive, or rejecting, we learn that relating with others is going to be difficult and unsatisfying. Not getting our emotional and physical needs fulfilled at a young age also creates trauma. It's no wonder that as an adult, Samantha still acted like a child seeking attention but only found the same rejection and insecurity because of a distant mother. And not surprisingly, Samantha's husband was distant and rejecting.

Mindfulness offers a means for transforming emotional entanglement by paying attention to the boundaries we have with others. When we become aware of our boundaries, we are in a position to question and to renegotiate them. Consider for a moment how any relationship — be it between nations, companies, or individuals — can be defined by the boundaries that are in place. Wars are often fought over boundaries. Samantha had poor boundaries with her mother; she allowed her mother to be abusive without providing her with any consequences. Samantha was unwilling to fight for her boundaries, by no longer calling her mother, for example, or limiting visits with her or negotiating what topics would be off-limits in their conversations. If we keep returning to a relationship that causes us pain and suffering, we need to take a closer look at our entanglement. Sometimes we will have to accept that certain people are not willing or are unable to respect or negotiate boundaries. Then we have a tough choice to make. How entangled are we willing to be? Establishing mindful boundaries can make a difference.

In my thirties, I decided to move away from Chicago to distance myself from the painful emotional entanglement I had with my father. A product of the Great Depression and World War II, my father was often abusively demanding, angry, and mistrustful. He rarely praised his children or showed affection, which of course created trauma. Even when I physically separated from my father, the entanglement continued to live within me and manifested itself in my personal and working relationships. I experienced a lot of personal frustration, but I did not recognize the root of my entanglement until my forties, when I entered into what appeared to be a promising business relationship.

After only a few months, my demanding, angry, and mistrustful business partner conspired to force me out of the business — and unbelievably, this event actually occurred on my father's birthday! The silver lining in all of this was that I did awaken and consciously began to explore and disentangle these emotions. As a result, I also oriented myself on my spiritual path. All thanks to my former business partner.

My journey of disentanglement is ongoing. It has meant taking on the responsibility of setting healthier, mindful boundaries in all my relationships. It has also helped me to forge a more forgiving and joyful relationship with my father. I'm no longer locked into the old push-and-pull, trying to get my needs met in an unsatisfying way. By freeing myself from previous trauma, I also freed my father from his old role. Thankfully, we have both evolved, and our relationship now encompasses kindness, interest, compassion, support, empathy, humor, and love.

Transforming emotional entanglement takes courage. Mindful boundary setting means standing up for ourselves, which is scary because we might be rejected. Being mindful of our emotions does not mean we hold them in a detached way that helps us escape emotions. Emotions are key to participating fully in life. "Flowers are restful to look at. They have neither emotions nor conflicts."[1] It's wonderful to be calm, as Freud points out in this quotation, but humans are not meant to be emotionless like flowers. Relationships are essential to our growth. When we are entangled in negative emotions, we are like a flower that isn't getting the nourishment it needs. To flourish, we need healthy emotional connections — giving us the space and boundaries to be ourselves, as well as the love and respect that nourish our soul.

Here is a beneficial step toward mindfully untangling gnarly emotional knots:

Accept that you have legitimate needs in an emotionally connected relationship. If you're not sure what those needs are, write them down. Let yourself feel good about being nourished emotionally and spiritually. Your list may include things such as the freedom to express your emotions, even displeasure, although not in a critical or blaming way; to ask for emotional support when you need it; to voice your desires. Affirm and practice expressing your legitimate needs. When the time comes, stand up for yourself. This takes courage and patience, so be kind as you let your authentic self be heard.

Notes

Epigraph. Oscar Wilde, "The Picture of Dorian Gray," in *The Collected Works of Oscar Wilde* (Hertfordshire, UK: Wordsworth, 2007), p. 31.

1.   Clare Cooper Marcus and Marni Barnes, eds., *Healing Gardens* (New Jersey: Wiley, 1999), p. 215.

40. Light Another's Candle

We make a living by what we get, but we make a life by what we give.

— WINSTON CHURCHILL

GENEROSITY — FREELY GIVING OF ONE'S SPIRIT, knowledge, and material goods — represents the best in humanity. It is here that we walk hand in hand with the divine, attuned with what Buddhist monk Thich Nhat Hanh calls "the truth of interbeing."[1] Generosity is at the top of Buddhism's list of Paramitas, or principles of enlightened living. In Judaism, the mitzvah is God's commandment to do good deeds. One of Islam's five pillars is zakat, or almsgiving. The Greek word *agape* has become part of our vernacular and refers to the highest form of charity and love for God's creation in Christian theology.

Where does charity begin? The seed for charity may be found by looking within at our own suffering and vulnerability. For indeed, who among us has not suffered some insult or hardship? Who could not benefit from being touched by love, kindness, and support?

Almost unbearable insults had already intruded on Eva Mozes Kor's life before she reached the age of ten, when her family was rounded up and crammed onto a stock car in a train bound for the concentration camp in Auschwitz during World War II. The long, dispiriting journey without food or water had been presaged in school, where Eva began to experience mistrust and fear. "We were going to school with teachers who were Nazi controlled and kids who beat us up," Eva recalled in a conversation with me.[2] "I was angry with my parents and anybody that had anything to do with life because I expected my parents to protect me, and my parents didn't and couldn't. My father prayed every day. And he said that if we did that, then everything would be okay. But things were getting worse and worse." As imaginative as children are, Eva could never have conjured the horror she was forced to experience.

Eva's family and hundreds of other weary prisoners on the train were met by the fearsome shouts and commands of machine gun–toting Nazi guards, their barking dogs, and the stench of incinerated bodies at the gates of a living hell. Less than thirty minutes after the prisoners were herded off the train, an SS guard noticed the close resemblance between Eva and her sister, Miriam. He ran about, yelling, "*Zwillinge!*" — the German word for "twins." The moment SS guards grabbed the twins, another quickly seized Eva's mother in his iron grip and dragged her in the opposite direction. She looked on hopelessly, sobbing with arms outstretched, while her children were pulled farther and farther away, at last disappearing into the crowd until all that remained were their piercing, fading cries.

More than sixty years later, Eva vividly remembers it all as if it happened yesterday. "I was ripped apart from the family, never to see them again. And there was no time to contemplate or process the event. I felt as if I was watching a picture happening to somebody else, like an out-of-body experience. The first night I couldn't sleep because there were rats on the floor. I went to the latrine and found the corpses of three children lying there. That was when I realized that this same thing could happen to Miriam and me unless I did something about it. I made a pledge, a silent promise to myself, right then. I said, *I will do anything so that Miriam and I will not end up on this filthy latrine floor.*"

It didn't take long for Eva to discover why she and Miriam, as well as scores of other twins, were being kept alive. She learned the truth shortly after being led to a barracks housing only girl twins. "Because we were twins, we were used in a variety of experiments. Three times a week, we were placed naked in a room, measured, and studied for six to eight hours. It was unbelievably demeaning." On the alternate days, Eva and Miriam were driven to a blood lab in Birkenau, where they were injected with germs and then had blood samples drawn. One twin was the experimental guinea pig, while the other served as the control. Should the experimental twin die, the healthy twin would be given a lethal heart injection and double autopsies would be performed to compare both "subjects." In order to conserve every ounce of energy and strength, the sisters rarely spoke.

"They took blood from one arm and gave us injections in the other," Eva recalls. "After one such injection, I became very ill and was taken to the hospital. Dr. Mengele came in the next day, looked at my fever chart, and declared that I had only two weeks to live. For the next two weeks, I was between life and death. I remember it was a struggle to crawl down the very long barracks to water at the other end. That was not something the supervisors would have been glad to see me do. I'm sure they didn't know why I was crawling. They knew I was delirious and semiconscious." Despite receiving no medical care, the physically fragile ten-year-old upheld the silent pledge of hope she made that first night in the latrine. "I never for one single moment for the nine months I was in Auschwitz ever saw myself dead. I always saw myself walking out of that camp. I never permitted for one brief moment fear and doubt to enter my mind. I didn't ever tell Miriam about it because she would have challenged me."

During Eva's darkest moment in the hospital, an unlikely source nourished her spirit and her body. One night in the unlit barracks, a slim figure moved stealthily down the long row of cots to the sick child's side. Eva looked up but could only see the silhouette of a woman staring down at her. The world stopped in that moment, and in the great silence between them, the silhouetted woman gently placed a morsel of bread on Eva's bed. The next night, the woman again glided like a ghost to Eva's side, never uttering a single word as she secretly set food beside Eva's head. On one occasion, the woman — likely a German supervisor — dared to bring a piece of chocolate cake. These small gifts from another helped Eva escape from what she now calls "the barracks of the living dead." That miracle of giving, along with her own dogged determination, helped Eva eventually recover and return to be with her sister.

But the experiments continued. After nine unrelenting months, hope appeared from an unlikely place. It literally came out of the sky. "One day an airplane came. I want you to realize that I was this ten-year-old kid, and I watched it with great interest. It was flying low enough that I could see an American flag on one of the wings. It made a circle over the camp and disappeared. The Nazis turned on the sirens, and then a larger group, maybe ten airplanes, flew by. I had hope because of those airplanes, and in my child's mentality, I thought all the world was a concentration camp. The bad guys were the Nazis and the good guys were the Americans, who were coming to save us. If I hadn't seen the airplanes in the sky, I don't know how much longer I could have survived. The more planes came, the more I understood that the good guys were winning and the bad guys were losing. By the end of November, there were no more experiments. They just stopped. So even in that isolated state of mind and deprivation, I could make some sense of what was going on. Those pilots gave me enough hope to survive one more day, to survive the experiments." Against all odds, Eva upheld her silent vow of hope for herself and Miriam. In a film of concentration-camp survivors leaving Auschwitz, Eva and her sister walk out of the gates at the absolute front of the line! Today, Eva says with conviction, "My life lesson is to never, ever give up, because when you give up, nothing happens. I learned that without hope, dying was very easy, and there were people who gave up."

Eva has used her own suffering as the means of reaching out to others in pain. She founded the CANDLES (Children of Auschwitz Nazi Deadly Lab Experiments Survivors) Holocaust Museum in Terre Haute, Indiana. After arsonists burned down the museum in 1993, Eva dedicated herself to rebuilding it, which she has done. Eva travels to schools throughout the world teaching forgiveness and healing from the pain of suffering and trauma. She offers hope to the next generation — and to all of us — through her selfless giving. What's more, her actions support the Buddha's counsel, "Thousands of candles can be lit from a single candle, and the life of the candle will not be shortened. Happiness never decreases by being shared."[3]

Here is a candle-lighting strategy you may find transformative.

Light another's candle this week by inspiring one person. It may help to look at your own personal wounds, struggles, and hardships. This takes courage, but it can also help you find your unique gift and discover how to share it. Many people who have struggled with addiction, for example, become addiction counselors. Can you think of a person — a teacher, a friend, a mentor, a relative, or anyone else — who made a positive impact on your life? How can you do the same for another?

Notes

Epigraph. Jack Canfield and Mark Victor Hansen, eds., *Chicken Soup for the Teacher's Soul* (Deerfield Beach, FL: HCI Books, 2002), p. 333.

1.   Thich Nhat Hanh, *Understanding Our Mind: 50 Verses on Buddhist Psychology* (Berkeley, CA: Parallax Press, 2006), p. 413.

2.   All quotes from Eva Mozes Kor are from a telephone interview with the author, July 4, 2007.

3.   "Buddha Quotes," http://thinkexist.com/quotation/thousands_of _candles_can_be_lighted_from_a_single/8680.html (accessed August 2009).

41. Attune Yourself to Others

*It is clear that if we are to live in harmony with ourselves
and with nature, we need to be able to communicate freely
in a creative movement in which no one permanently
holds to or otherwise defends his own ideas.*

— DAVID BOHM

HAVE YOU EVER ENGAGED IN A HEATED POLITICAL or religious discussion that created misunderstanding or ill will? This happens all too often because our style of communication leads to conflict. Enhancing attunement, on the other hand, is a means of mindfully looking within in order to join with another and gain greater understanding. Interestingly, the word *discussion* is derived from the same root as the words *concussion* and *percussion*. Discussion, in other words, is a dialectical method of argument in which we bang loudly on someone with our opinions, our egocentric perceptions, and our desire to be right. This method may resolve some issues, but it cannot bring us closer. Fortunately, the option of attunement opens the door to a more enlightened and aware form of communication. With attunement, we can become skilled at building bridges of peace and tolerance.

Giving in to or pleasing others in order to avoid conflict is not attunement. For example, Janice, a young woman I worked with, so wanted her relationship to work that she altered her life to fit her boyfriend's lifestyle. Whereas she used to wake up early in the morning to practice yoga and meditation, Janice now slept until midmorning, when her boyfriend would slowly awaken. She used to eat what she felt was a healthy vegetarian diet and drank wine in moderation. But now Janice consumed the fattening foods and meats her boyfriend enjoyed, and she drank more to match his love for wine and beer. Janice used to hike, bike, and go to movies; with her boyfriend, she instead stayed home and watched TV. Eventually, Janice realized she was giving up too much of herself just to be in a relationship.

There are many aspects to mindful attunement, and these can be expressed both verbally and nonverbally. Verbal attunement starts with openness, a willingness to enter another's worldview in order to understand them. This can be accomplished with dialogue, as opposed to discussion. Dialogue, which can be translated as "through word," is based on the foundation that all ideas are vulnerable. This means that my ideas and your ideas are vulnerable (not just the other person's) and that our ideas must be suspended for dialogue to occur. Dialogue requires and develops a shared desire to seek truth by sharing ideas. This is quite different from persuading someone to adopt a particular belief system.

In dialogue, skillfulness with words is vital and is reflected in the use of nonblaming and nonjudgmental language. This means setting aside, if only for a few moments at a time, our own strongly held opinions and preconceptions. Verbal attunement allows another to feel heard and validated, and it builds the shared sense of we. Dialogue promotes a give-and-take in communication, with different perspectives providing another ample time to express. Attunement in dialogue also requires clarification, which means we listen first and try to make sense of what was said by asking questions afterward. Verbal attunement also involves reflecting back to the other what was heard, without interpretation, to confirm what was said. Maintaining a respectful tone and intensity of voice are also aspects of attunement. Flat speech and negative tones do not reflect attunement. When we strive to offer a high level of verbal awareness, we are also showing an appreciation for the singularity of another's mind.

Suspending our beliefs in order to create dialogue is no easy task, however. We will need to draw upon the mindfulness of mind and body to notice when the body clenches and when the mind anxiously does backflips upon hearing a perspective radically opposed to our own. Nonverbal attunement skills come into play at this point. As described earlier (in chapter 38, "Seek Out Happy and Meaningful Connections"), mirror neurons enable us to attune ourselves to another, so the more we can cool down our emotional core and limbic system, the more we can facilitate the calming of another's. Diaphragmatic breathing and an awareness of the emotions and tension present in the body are valuable aids. Breathe into the parts of the body that clench, tighten, or tense, and exhale these away. We find our center as we continue to listen and tune in.

Nonverbal attunement is expressed primarily through facial expressions, body language, the tone and intensity of voice, and touch. Do you make consistent eye contact while speaking? The understanding of eye contact varies among cultures, so it is always important to learn about this when we hope to share dialogue with someone from a different culture. Of course, smiling, like any open facial expression, is a powerful way to reduce reactivity in others. Body language can do this as well. Become aware of your body posture when you want to attune yourself to another. Are your arms crossed or open? Are you nodding or shaking your head? Are you rolling your eyes or fidgeting? When we become sensitive to nonverbal cues, we can communicate nonviolent responses through nonaggressive gestures. The intensity and tone of voice are also aspects of nonverbal communication. Is the tone of your voice respectful? Is the intensity in another's voice aggressive or welcoming? We can also match our vocal intensity to another person's to promote closeness — matching the excitement or the quiet, for example, in another's emotional state.

Paying attention when we feel close to another person is a good way to become more aware of this nonverbal process. Finally, touch increases the production of oxytocin, a bonding hormone in the brain's core that correlates to various levels of trust we experience in social interactions. Physical touch also reduces the level of cortisol in the body, which improves mood and reduces stress. When appropriate, a handshake, a hug, or a sympathetic hand on the shoulder can balance another's feelings of internal stress.

Attunement, like mindfulness, is a skill that needs to be practiced and developed. Give the following exercise a try for building intimacy.

Practice attuning yourself to family and friends with these five nonverbal cues:

1. Make eye contact.
2. Assume an open, nonthreatening body posture.
3. Use an appropriate form of touch.
4. Smile and present an open facial expression.
5. Look within to find empathy.

These touchstones will help you create a safe and accepting environment, where others feel safe to express themselves.

Note

Epigraph. David Bohm, *On Dialogue* (London and New York: Routledge, 1996), p. 4.

42. Offer Up Your Nonjudgment and Joy

I do not judge the universe.

— THE DALAI LAMA

*I*MAGINE FOR A MOMENT HOW DIFFERENT YOUR LIFE might be if you had never been weighed down by the judgments and the demands of others, including everything from parental pressures and expectations to cultural standards. How would it feel to be understood and supported for the person you are instead of being measured by outer accomplishments? Imagine having family and friends who do not want to exert control over your grades, jobs, or other life choices, who instead appreciate and understand your need to make your own decisions. What would it be like to spend time with people more interested in sharing their joy, love, goodness, and happiness with you, as well as their happiness *for* you, than their struggles, cynicism, and pain?

Spend a few moments imagining what this would be like. Let the feelings of support and joy sink into all the cells of your body. It is important to experience and value this kind of connection with others. What is this feeling? It is the sympathetic joy that grows out of nonjudgmental compassion. Why not offer it to others as well? In the offering, we become the joy and lightness we seek.

"I can think of a thousand things that I don't like about my daughter," exclaims Marty, a sixty-three-year-old auto mechanic with silver-gray hair and a square jaw. "I don't like that she smokes, she's an alcoholic, she keeps her home messy, and she's always asking me for money." I learn there is a lot more to Marty's list of disappointments. In particular, he is infuriated by the way his daughter and her husband use their children to manipulate his grandfatherly heartstrings and borrow money — "which never gets repaid." Listening to Marty's story, I don't blame him for being angry and upset. But it's also obvious to me that Marty's judgmental view of his daughter is making him miserable and harming his relationship with her.

Over time, Marty warms up to the idea that he can accept his daughter for who she is and at the same time set compassionate boundaries. She can make her own life decisions and pay her own way. When Marty lets go of his anger and unrealistic expectations, his relationship with his daughter begins to thaw and becomes more honest and open. On the day we wrap up our final session, Marty reports with a big grin, "Things are great. My daughter called me up from the car dealership to ask me about a car she was buying. I let her know that I trusted her decision and that I wouldn't be helping out. I never thought that accepting her for who she is would make such a difference."

Being judgmental is not the same as being discriminating and discerning and not the same as evaluating and analyzing in order to arrive at a decision or to make comparisons. A judgmental mind can be a dangerous thing. It gets stuck in a personal and limited perspective of I-me-mine. Holding people to black-and-white standards leaves little allowance for the quirks that make us who we are. In contrast, a joyful and compassionate mind invites hope and makes life bearable. An innate joy that lives in all of us wants to break out of its seed of separateness and aloneness. The joyful mind is not obsessed with winning or needing to be right. It is more interested in sharing joy and being connected. The compassionate mind reaps joy by giving and spreading joy, even in unlikely and unexpected places.

Even if the expansiveness of joy and compassion has eluded you, new brain research shows that when we practice thinking compassionate thoughts, we change the brain in positive ways. In one of the cutting-edge studies led by Richard Davidson, a research professor and director of the Lab for Affective Neuroscience at the University of Wisconsin at Madison, a group of eight Buddhist monks and long-term meditation practitioners showed dramatic changes in their brains while practicing a compassion and loving-kindness meditation. With 128 sensors from an electroencephalogram (EEG) attached to their heads, the subjects were instructed to let thoughts of compassion permeate their minds without focusing on any particular person or object. The researchers defined compassion as an "unrestricted readiness and availability to help living beings." Compared to the control group, the long-term practitioners of meditation and compassion showed a significant increase in gamma brain wave activity, a higher amplification of gamma waves, and gamma waves that were synchronized in parts of the brain. Gamma brain waves are implicated in memory, improved problem solving, enhanced brain function, higher levels of happiness — and, according to this study, higher levels of compassion.[1]

Yes, compassion is about opening the heart to share suffering and tenderness, but its flip side is about sharing lightheartedness and joy. Sometimes, however, we manage to get serious and judgmental about not being light and joyful enough! Buddhist teacher Pema Chödrön points out, "In addition to a sense of humor, a basic support for a joyful mind is curiosity, paying attention, taking an interest in the world around you. You don't actually have to be happy. But being curious without a heavy judgmental attitude helps. If you *are* judgmental, you can be curious about that."[2] What is your level of compassion readiness? How available are you in this moment — and this next one — to notice judgment and expectation of yourself and others? Are you ready to seek joy and appreciation for others in this moment?

Also, share your humor, foibles, and insights with others. I remember one time in the monastery when I took a fresh pot of hot tea and placed it on a small table next to the kitchen. The table was already unsteady, and while sitting down I placed my hands on the table, causing it to give way entirely. As the table literally split in half, I crashed onto the floor with hot tea spilling and scalding me. A monk who was in the next room came running when he heard the crash. This must have been quite a sight, for when he saw me we both started laughing.

Though I was in pain, I let go of my embarrassment and self-judgment in that moment, and all that was left was the humor in the situation. Sometimes our foibles can create joyful moments — whether intended or not. Make yourself available for the joy of compassion.

Find a quiet place where you can sit and focus on thoughts and feelings of compassion. For several minutes, repeat the words "May I be available and ready to help all living beings. May I share my joy and lightness with others, and may I let others share this with me." Eventually, think about those who are suffering, and picture yourself helping to reduce their suffering through acts of joy.

Notes

Epigraph. Fabrizio Didonna, ed., *Clinical Handbook of Mindfulness* (New York: Springer, 2008), p. 221.

1. Antoine Lutz, Lawrence L. Greischar, Nancy B. Rawlings, Matthieu Ricard, and Richard J. Davidson, "Long-Term Meditators Self-Induce High-Amplitude Gamma Synchrony during Mental Practice," *Proceedings of the National Academy of Sciences* 101, no. 46, November 16, 2004, www.pnas.org/content/101/46/16369.full.pdf+html (accessed June 2009).

2. Pema Chödrön, *Start Where You Are: A Guide to Compassionate Living* (Boston: Shambhala, 2004), p. 133.

43. Cultivate Kind Speech

Kindness is the language which the deaf can hear and the blind can see.

— MARK TWAIN

W HAT'S IN A WORD? Unlike in mathematics, where one plus one equals two no matter how many times the numbers are added up, communication and expression are subtle, diverse, and complex. The same word or sentence can possess multiple shades of meaning. And the emotion and energy behind words depend on the context as well as on our personal associations and histories with them.

In his book *Unfolding Meaning*, physicist David Bohm explores how thought and language contain the form of "unbroken wholeness." Words and meaning, he says, are part of an implicate, or enfolded, order that mirrors the interconnected universe. So, every verbal expression we use, even those with a simple message, contains many levels of meaning and enfoldment. According to Bohm, emotions and feelings enfold thought. Thought enfolds intention. Intention enfolds consciousness.

Consciousness enfolds connection with source, and so on, in a chain of enfoldments.[1] In this paradigm, language possesses an indivisible wholeness that spreads outward like ripples in a pond.

The Sufi mystic Hazrat Inayat Khan writes, "Since all things are made by the power of sound, of vibration, so every thing is made by a portion thereof, and man can create his world by the same power. . . . This knowledge acts as wings for a man; it helps him to rise from earth to heaven, and he can penetrate through the life seen and unseen."[2] Knowing that our words can either heal or hurt, we can strive to use words mindfully and wisely — thus elevating daily language from the mundane to the spiritual.

Jane, a stylishly dressed woman in her fifties, has come to see me because she often goes "ballistic" with people in her life. I notice that she is quick to laugh and smile. No one would guess on first meeting that Jane can get so angry that she loses control over her words and her screaming results in the other person hanging up the phone or leaving the room. And it isn't just adults that Jane bombards with her harsh language. "It really hurts me that I do this with my children," she says. Jane also worries that she has put up a wall between herself and her husband, who has physically and emotionally withdrawn from her.

I learn that Jane's stress levels are extremely high. Between working as a sales rep and homeschooling her children, she has scarce time to decompress. She is also experiencing menopause, which adversely affects her moods. Eventually, Jane creates a plan that includes boundaries and downtime to reduce stress. She also learns how to deescalate her language and express her emotions to her husband before they reach ballistic levels. A naturopathic doctor helps her regulate hormones and prescribes a precursor for serotonin and dopamine. Jane notices the differences immediately. Not only is her husband talking with her again, but she feels more self-control and is more nurturing with her children.

Words are like a living clay with which we shape our relationships. Wise speech can build trust; unkind speech can cause enduring damage. In our electronic age, words travel faster than ever before. Email messages are often written quickly and risk being misunderstood and misinterpreted. To avoid confusion, some companies now require employees to communicate by phone or in person. Technology is complicating our effective use of language itself, an already complex system. A greater awareness of how to use words with skill and kindness is more important than ever. Where do we begin?

According to the Buddha, a statement is only proper and kind when, "It is spoken at the right time. It is spoken in truth. It is spoken affectionately. It is spoken beneficially. It is spoken with a mind of goodwill. "[3] A statement containing these five elements exemplifies kind speech. Let's take a closer look at the first condition, speaking at the right time. Speaking at the right time sometimes means *not* speaking, such as when we are feeling upset and reactive. This aspect of kind speech means that forbearance, the capacity for restraint, may be more important than saying what's on your mind in a given moment. Forbearance is a kind of grace we give others. It's a sign of patience and wisdom to know when your message will be heard

and valued. We might refrain, for example, from telling someone who was just laid off about the incredible promotion we
were given. Being in the present moment, we learn to trust the
feeling in the body to help us know when the time is right for
speaking.

Truthfulness is the next element of kind speech. Honesty is
the cornerstone of speaking kindly because it builds trust. Honesty requires that we remove barriers to honest speech, such as
greed, envy, selfishness, hatred, and other personal desires to
gain advantage. Lying undermines social trust and cohesion.
As lies proliferate they get harder and harder to contain. Dis-
content, unrest, and war are often fueled by forms of lies, such
as slander and rumor, that dehumanize others. Truthful and
honest speech, however, provides us with a link to reality, to
seeing things as they are. Be alert and careful, though, that so-
called truthful speech is not really mean-spirited speech that is
being rationalized and disguised as honesty. Have you ever
heard someone say, "I'm just being honest," after they have
clearly been unkind? There are many ways to practice genuine
truthful speech. All are effective only when the spirit of kind
instruction has not been forgotten.

The third aspect of kind speech is to speak with affection,
or with a gentle tone. This means you not only think about
what you say but also pay particular attention to *how* you say
the words. Are your words congruent with your feelings? If
you are upset about something but act as if nothing is wrong,
then your speech is not true. How can you speak in a way that
is not harsh and that conveys compassion? Thich Nhat Hanh,
Vietnamese poet and monk, says this about choosing the right
words: "Consider each word carefully before you say anything,

so that your speech is 'Right' in both form and content. . . . You have a right to tell another everything that is in your heart with the condition that you use only loving speech. If you are not able to speak calmly, then don't speak that day."[4] This means speaking without anger, blame, criticism, and name calling. Even a complaint about something can be expressed respectfully, without resorting to blame and character assassination.

The fourth facet of kind speech — to use words in a beneficial way — asks us to remember that speech is not a weapon to be used to hurt, shame, or blame another who may have hurt us. It is a genuine expression of how we feel in this moment, expressed with compassion, patience, and kindness. Using speech beneficially also implies using words carefully, such as by avoiding gossip or pointless conversations. I know of one workplace in which the employees agreed not to speak about anyone unless that person was present. The result — according to one employee — was a healthier work environment without gossip and unnecessary talk.

The final aspect of kind speech is to speak with goodwill, which means to speak with intention and from the heart. This form of speech fosters friendship, deepens understanding, and is nonjudgmental and nonblaming. Speaking in this way doesn't mean you can't be assertive, but it does mean that you avoid bullying and aggressive language. When you communicate with a sense of goodwill, all parties feel heard and respected. Also, it doesn't mean you can't defend yourself if you are abused or treated badly. The Buddha himself was once verbally abused. He responded by saying that when a gift is offered, the receiver can choose not to accept it. In this way, the Buddha refused and returned the unwanted abuse.

Don't judge yourself harshly when you speak less skillfully or less kindly than you would like — kind speech takes a lifetime of practice. Here is one technique for cultivating it.

At the end of each day, take time to reflect on the interactions in which your words were less than totally transparent, honest, and kind. Make the effort to honestly assess the reasons and emotions behind your speech. Forgive yourself for the times that you spoke out of greed, anger, or another unhealthy emotion. Vow to improve upon these in the future.

Notes

Epigraph. John P. Holms and Karin Baji, eds., *Bite-Size Twain* (New York: St. Martin's, 1998), p. 16.

1. David Bohm, *Unfolding Meaning: A Weekend of Dialogue with David Bohm*, ed. Donald Factor (New York: Routledge, 1985).

2. Hazrat Inayat Khan, *The Mysticism of Sound and Music* (Boston: Shambhala, 1996), p. 27.

3. "Right Speech, Meaning and Significance on the Eightfold Path," www.hinduwebsite.com/buddhism/rightspeech.asp (accessed June 2009).

4. Thich Nhat Hanh, *The Heart of the Buddha's Teaching* (Boston: Shambhala, 1996), p. 89.

44. Mind Your Relationships

A wonderful fact to reflect upon, that every human creature is constituted to be that profound secret and mystery to every other.

— CHARLES DICKENS

RELATIONSHIPS ARE OFTEN CONFOUNDING. The desire to repair and understand relationships leads many of us to self-help books and therapy. Mindfulness, on the other hand, doesn't promise to solve long-standing family issues, it isn't a prescription for getting the relationship we want, and just because we are practicing mindfulness does not mean others will embrace it with us. Of course, secretly hoping that others will solve "their" problems this way with us is understandable. It would be nice, but mindfulness in relationships is about not what we can get but what we can give.

Awareness of what we bring to others is something within our power, no matter what. The Dalai Lama says, "If there is love, there is hope to have real families, real brotherhood, real equanimity, real peace. If the love within your mind is lost, if you continue to see other beings as enemies, then no matter how much knowledge or education you have, no matter how much material progress is made, only suffering and confusion will ensue."[1] To be mindful in relationships means to accept people just as they are while taking responsibility for those things that we can change: our mind and our heart, with our capacity to trust and love.

Susan is a forty-four-year-old mother of three who has always had a difficult relationship with her mother. Susan is sure she knows what the problem is: "She's always trying to tell me how to raise my kids. It's always something. Either I'm not making them the right kind of food or I'm giving them too much of the right food. I just can't win." It's clear that Susan has a fixed mind-set when it comes to her mother. Fixed mind-sets can be limiting, if not harmful.

One day, I give Susan a homework assignment. "The next time you talk with your mother on the phone, I want you to keep your eyes shut. I want you to listen intently to her voice. Pay attention to what is really there, not to words that trigger an ancient script in your head. If she expresses concern, hear the concern. If she expresses curiosity, just hear the curiosity." When Susan returns, she explains that her mother didn't badger or criticize her on the phone. For the first time in years, she heard a woman who was lonely and who wanted to make a con- nection. By letting go of the old mind-set, Susan made space for what was actually present. This, in turn, allowed Susan to act differently; she was not automatically defensive or judgmental of her mother. Susan opened her mind and heart and accepted her mother, and they are now developing a satisfying and more adult relationship.

Being mindful in relationships can be difficult, especially because it often reveals the truth of the relationships. What do we do when we learn that our partner isn't caring or committed to the relationship? We can deny the truth and construct a fantasy relationship, or we can apply mindfulness to see and fully accept a relationship for what it is — without blaming or judging the relationship or the other person involved. Once freed from our judgment, this person, too, may become more open and less resentful. In relationships, as in all systems in nature, a change in one part of the system affects the whole system. Intentionally Centering Attention Now lets us notice the changes and appreciate them for the treasures they bring, recognizing that relationships are fragile and impermanent. Tend to each person in your life as you would an acorn you plant. Water and nurture that seedling without expectations, and let it grow into the oak tree it is meant to be.

Now that you have learned the relationship key, you can review its teachings and choose one to use for an entire week. Then move on to another the next week. The following strategy applies to all the relationship teachings.

Make a point of consciously imagining each person you meet as your own brother or sister — someone whose well-being, safety, health, and happiness you deeply care about. See how this changes your perspective and willingness to offer kindness and compassion. Also, notice how this changes the nature of the relationship.

Having completed the final teaching of *The Mindfulness Code,* I hope you find yourself not at the end but at the beginning of an inspiring and joyful journey. It is a journey we can carry with us — in mind, body, heart, spirit, and relationship — wherever we go.

May you be inspired.
May you be brave, strong, and enduring,
and may you walk this path to its end.

— U PANDITA[2]

Notes

Epigraph. Charles Dickens, *A Tale of Two Cities* (New York: Bantam Classics, 1989), p. 11.

1. Dalai Lama, *The Path to Tranquility: Daily Wisdom* (New York: Penguin, 2002), p. 29.

2. U Pandita, *In This Very Life: The Liberation Teachings of the Buddha* (Boston: Wisdom Publications, 1992), p. 131.

Acknowledgments

*T*HERE HAVE BEEN MANY who have contributed to this
book. My heartfelt appreciation extends to all those individuals throughout history who have dedicated themselves to
awakening through mindfulness and who have shared that
knowledge with others.

In particular, my late teacher, the Venerable U Silananda,
who for years was a tireless mindfulness guide to seekers; Ashin
Thitzana, my spiritual monk brother, for sharing his deep wisdom and knowledge of Buddhist writings; U Thondara and the
monks and community of the Burma Buddhist Monastery;
Randy Fitzgerald, a coconspirator in all things having to do
with writing, for his generous sharing of ideas and feedback;
Greg Crosby, for joyfully offering his creativity, encouragement, and intuition, as well as for sharing his wise and enlightened teachings with many; Robert Biswas-Diener for sharing
stories of hope and happiness; fellow board members of The
Center for Mindful Eating for their immense heart and support,
as well as their extraordinary efforts toward reducing suffering in the world — Roshi Jan Chozen Bays, Megrette Fletcher,
Ronna Kabatznick, Jean Kristeller, Gretchen Newmark, Brian
Shelley, Ronald Thebarge, and Char Wilkins; Bill Gladstone,

my agent, for his wholehearted support of this project; Georgia Hughes, editorial director at New World Library, for her thoughtful insights and suggestions, and a desire to make a positive change in the world through the written word; Kristen Cashman from New World Library and Vesela Simic for their wonderful editorial gifts, which have enhanced these pages. Also, my thanks extends to numerous others — including friends, teachers, colleagues, clients, acquaintances, students, and so on — with whom I had the pleasure of exploring and learning more about mindfulness. May we together continue to discover the healing power of mindfulness.

I am deeply grateful to my family's generous spirit — in particular, the deep compassion of my sister, Cynthia; the laughter of my brother, Jim; and the kind words of support from my father, Norman. Especially I want to express deep gratitude to my mother, Barbara, and my wife, Sanda — the love of my life — for understanding and encouraging my journey into mindfulness. May all beings be inspired to take this peaceful journey of awakening.

Bibliography and Resources

Books

Altman, Donald. *Art of the Inner Meal*. Portland, OR: Moon Lake Media, 2002.

———. *Living Kindness*. Portland, OR: Moon Lake Media, 2003.

———. *Meal by Meal*. Novato, CA: New World Library, 2004.

Andreasen, Nancy. *The Creating Brain*. Washington, DC: Dana Press, 2005.

Ashley-Farrand, Thomas. *Healing Mantras*. New York: Ballantine, 1999.

Atwan, Robert, George Dardass, and Peggy Rosenthal, eds. *Divine Inspiration*. New York: Oxford University Press, 1997.

Baer, Ruth A., ed. *Mindfulness-Based Treatment Approaches*. Burlington, MA: Elsevier Academic Press, 2006.

Begley, Sharon. *Train Your Brain, Change Your Mind*. New York: Ballantine Books, 2007.

Bhikkhu, Buddhadasa. *Heartwood of the Bodhi Tree*. Boston: Wisdom Publications, 1994.

Blakney, R. B. *The Way of Life*. New York: Signet Classics, 2001.

Bohm, David. *On Dialogue*. London and New York: Routledge, 1996.

Brantley, Jeffrey. *Calming Your Anxious Mind*. Oakland, CA: New Harbinger Publications, 2007.

Byrom, Thomas. *Dhammapada*. Boston: Shambhala, 1993.

Campbell, Joseph. *The Power of Myth*. With Bill Moyers. New York: Broadway, 1988.

Canfield, Jack, and Mark Victor Hansen. *Chicken Soup for the Teacher's Soul*. Deerfield Beach, FL: HCI Books, 2002.

Chödrön, Pema. *Start Where You Are.* Boston: Shambhala, 2004.

Chozen Bays, Jan. *Mindful Eating.* Boston: Shambhala, 2009.

Coleman, Mark. *Awake in the Wild.* Novato, CA: New World Library, 2006.

Coppieters, Frank. *Handbook for the Evolving Heart.* Prescott, AZ: Conflux Press, 2006.

Cousineau, Phil. *Once and Future Myths.* Boston: Conari Press, 2001.

Cousins, Norman. *Anatomy of an Illness.* New York: W. W. Norton, 2001.

Daiensai, Richard Kirsten. *Smile.* London: M Q Publications, 2004.

Dalai Lama and Howard C. Cutler. *The Art of Happiness.* New York: Riverhead, 1998.

Dalai Lama. *Live in a Better Way.* Edited by Renuka Singh. New York: Penguin Books, 2002.

———. *The Path to Tranquility.* New York: Penguin Books, 2002.

Darling, David J. *The Universal Book of Mathematics.* Hoboken, NJ: John Wiley & Sons, 2004.

Das, Lama Surya. *Awakening the Buddha Within.* New York: Broadway Books, 1997.

Didonna, Fabrizio, ed. *Clinical Handbook of Mindfulness.* New York: Springer, 2008.

Diener, Ed, and Robert Biswas-Diener. *Happiness.* New York: Wiley, 2008.

Dossey, Larry. *Healing Words.* San Francisco: HarperSanFrancisco, 1994.

Durston, Diane. *Wabi Sabi.* North Adams, MA: Storey Publishing, 2006.

Easwaran, Eknath. *The Mantram Handbook.* Petaluma, CA: Nilgiri Press, 1977.

Gerrard, Don. *One Bowl.* Cambridge, MA: Da Capo Press, 2001.

Goleman, Daniel. *Destructive Emotions.* New York: Bantam Books, 2003.

Gordon, James. *Unstuck.* New York: Penguin Books, 2008.

Hanh, Thich Nhat. *The Heart of the Buddha's Teaching.* Boston: Shambhala, 1996.

———. *The Miracle of Mindfulness.* Boston: Beacon Press, 1987.

———. *Peace Is Every Step.* New York: Bantam Books, 1992.

Heschel, Abraham Joshua. *The Sabbath*. New York: Farrar, Strauss, & Giroux, 1996.

Joyce, James. *Dubliners*. Edited by Margaret Norris. New York: Oxford University Press, 2008.

Kabat-Zinn, Jon. *Full Catastrophe Living*. New York: Bantam Dell, 1990.

———. *Wherever You Go There You Are*. New York: Hyperion, 1997.

Kabat-Zinn, Myla, and Jon Kabat-Zinn. *Everyday Blessings*. New York: Hyperion, 1998.

Kabatznick, Ronna. *The Zen of Eating*. New York: Perigree Trade, 1998.

Kaplan, Aryeh. *Jewish Meditation*. New York: Schocken Books, 1985.

Kass, Amy, ed. *Giving Well, Doing Good*. Bloomington: Indiana University Press, 2007.

Khan, Hazrat Inayat. *The Mysticism of Sound and Music*. Boston: Shambhala, 1996.

Klein, Allen. *The Healing Power of Humor*. New York: Tarcher, 1989.

Kornfield, Jack. *The Art of Forgiveness, Loving-Kindness, and Peace*. New York: Bantam Books, 2002.

Kraybill, Donald. *Old Order Amish*. Photographs by Lucian Niemeyer. Baltimore: Johns Hopkins University Press, 1993.

Langer, Ellen. *Mindfulness*. Cambridge, MA: Da Capo Press, 1990.

Laozi, and Archie J. Bahm. *Tao Teh King*. World Books, 1986.

Libet, Benjamin. *Mind Time*. Cambridge, MA: Harvard University Press, 2005.

Lyubomirsky, Sonja. *The How of Happiness*. New York: Penguin Books, 2008.

Mahasi, Sayadaw. *Fundamentals of Vipassana Meditation*. Berkeley, CA: Dhammachakka Meditation Center, 1991.

Maitreya, Balangoda Ananda. The Dhammapada. Berkeley, CA: Parallax Press, 1995.

Marcus, Clare Cooper, and Marni Barnes, eds. *Healing Gardens*. New York: Wiley, 1999.

McDermott, Diane. *Making Hope Happen*. Oakland, CA: New Harbinger Publications, 1999.

McDermott, Diane, and C. R. Snyder. *The Great Big Book of Hope*. Oakland, CA: New Harbinger Publications, 2000.

Merton, Thomas. *New Seeds of Contemplation*. New York: New Directions, 1961.

Mikulincer, Mario, and Philip Shaver. *Attachment in Adulthood*. New York: Guilford Press, 2007.

Moring, Gary F. *The Complete Idiot's Guide to Understanding Einstein*. New York: Penguin Books, 2004.

Mother Teresa. *The Joy in Loving*. New York: Penguin Books, 2000.

Muir, John. *The Yosemite*. San Francisco: Sierra Club Books, 1988.

O'Connor, Richard. *Undoing Perpetual Stress*. New York: Berkley Trade, 2006.

O'Donohue, John. *Anam Cara*. New York: Harper Perennial, 2004.

————. *Eternal Echoes*. New York: Harper Perennial, 2002.

Pandita, Sayadaw U. *In This Very Life*. Boston: Wisdom Publications, 1992.

Phillips, Jan. *Divining the Body*. Woodstock, VT: Skylight Paths Publishing, 2005.

Ricard, Matthieu. *Happiness*. New York: Little Brown, 2007.

Rilke, Rainer Maria. *Book of Hours*. Translated by Anita Barrows and Joanna Macy. New York: Riverhead Trade, 1997.

Rinpoche, Sogyal. *The Spirit of Buddhism*. New York: HarperOne, 2003.

Rumi, Jalal al-Din. *Essential Rumi*. Translated by Coleman Barks. New York: HarperOne, 1997.

Ryals, Steve. *Drunk with Wonder*. Ukiah, CA: Rock Creek Press, 2006.

Salzberg, Sharon. *Loving-Kindness*. Boston: Shambhala, 1997.

Sapolsky, Robert. *Why Zebras Don't Get Ulcers*. New York: W. H. Freeman, 1994.

Schwartz, Barry. *Paradox of Choice*. New York: Harper Perennial, 2004.

Schwartz, Jeffrey, and Sharon Begley. *The Mind and the Brain*. New York: Harper Perennial, 2003.

Seigel, Daniel, and Mary Hartzell. *Parenting from the Inside Out*. New York: Tarcher, 2003.

Seligman, Martin. *Learned Optimism*. New York: Vintage, 2006.

Sen XV, Soshitsu. *Tea Life, Tea Mind*. New York & Tokyo: Weatherhill, 1995.

Silananda, Venerable U. *Four Foundations of Mindfulness*. Boston: Wisdom Publications, 1990.

Skach-Mills, Daniel. *The Tao of Now*. Portland, OR: KenArnoldBooks, 2008.

Snyder, C. R. *The Handbook of Hope*. New York: Academic Press, 2000.

———. *The Psychology of Hope*. New York: Free Press, 2003.

Snyder, C. R., Diane McDermott, William Cook, and Michael A. Rapoff. *Hope for the Journey*. New York: Basic Books, 1997.

Tart, Charles. *Living the Mindful Life*. Boston: Shambhala, 1994.

Thoreau, Henry David. *Walden and Other Writings*. Boston: Adamant Media, 2000.

Tolle, Eckhart. *A New Earth*. New York: Penguin, 2008.

Trungpa, Chögyam. *Shambhala*. Boston: Shambhala, 1988.

Tutu, Desmond. *No Future Without Forgiveness*. New York: Doubleday, 1999.

Twain, Mark. *Bite-Size Twain*. Edited by John P. Holmes and Karin Baji. New York: St. Martin's, 1998.

Tzu, Lao. *Tao Te Ching*. Translated by Stephen Mitchell. New York: Harper Perennial, 2006.

Watson, Lyall. *Gifts of Unknown Things*. Rochester, VT: Destiny Books, 1991.

Whybrow, Peter. *American Mania*. New York: W. W. Norton, 2006.

Wilde, Oscar. *Collected Works of Oscar Wilde*. Hertfordshire, UK: Wordsworth, 2007.

Williams, Mark, John Teasdale, Zindel Segal, and Jon Kabat-Zinn. *The Mindful Way through Depression*. New York: Guilford Press, 2007.

Scientific Papers and Book Chapters

Bennett, Mary, Janice Zeller, Lisa Rosenberg, and Judith McCann. "The Effect of Mirthful Laughter on Stress and Natural Killer Cell Activity." *Alternative Therapies* 9, no. 2 (2003): 39–44.

Creswell, J. David, Baldwin M. Way, Naomi I. Eisenberger, and Matthew D. Lieberman. "Neural Correlates of Dispositional Mindfulness during Affect Labeling." *Psychosomatic Medicine* 69 (2007): 560–65.

Davidson, Richard, Jon Kabat-Zinn, et al. "Alterations in Brain and Immune Function Produced by Mindulness Meditation." *Psychosomatic Medicine* 65 (2003): 564–70.

Kabat-Zinn, Jon, Leslie Lipworth, and Robert Burney. "The Clinical

Use of Mindfulness Meditation for the Self-Regulation of Chronic Pain." *Journal of Behavioral Medicine* 8, no. 2 (1985): 163–90.

Kabat-Zinn, Massion, Kristeller, Peterson, et al. "Effectiveness of a Meditation-Based Stress Reduction Program in the Treatment of Anxiety Disorders." *American Journal of Psychiatry* 149 (1992): 936–43.

Moore, S. L. "Hope Makes a Difference." *Journal of Psychiatric and Mental Health Nursing* 12, no. 1 (2005): 100–105.

Roth, Beth, and Tracy Creaser. "Mindfulness Meditation-Based Stress Reduction: Experience with a Bilingual Inner-City Program." *The Nurse Practitioner* 22, no. 3 (1997): 150–52, 154, 157.

Santorelli, S. F. "Mindfulness and Mastery in the Workplace." In *Engaged Buddhist Reader*. Berkeley, CA: Parallax Press, 1996.

Website Resources

Donald Altman's websites: www.mindfulpractices.com and www.mindfulnesscode.com

Antihunger and antipoverty organizations: http://www.bread.org/learn/links.html

The Center for Mindful Eating: www.TCME.org

Center for Mindfulness and Psychotherapy: www.mindfulnessandpsychotherapy.org

Center for Mindfulness in Medicine, Healthcare, and Society: www.umassmed.edu/content.aspx?id=41252

Dana Foundation: www.dana.org

Hope Foundation: www.hopefoundation.org

Laboratory for Affective Neuroscience, University of Wisconsin at Madison: http://psyphz.psych.wisc.edu/

Social Cognitive Neuroscience Laboratory, UCLA: www.scn.ucla.edu

Index

About the Author

*D*ONALD ALTMAN, MA, LPC, is a practicing psychotherapist, former Buddhist monk, award-winning writer, and board member of The Center for Mindful Eating (TCME.org). He is an adjunct professor at Lewis and Clark College Graduate School and is on the faculty of the Interpersonal Neurobiology program at Portland State University.

Donald conducts mindful living and mindful eating workshops and retreats around the nation and is known as America's Mindfulness Coach for the way he makes mindful living and spiritual values accessible in daily life. Donald trained with the Venerable U Silananda, author of *The Four Foundations of Mindfulness,* at a Buddhist monastery located near the San Bernardino Mountains in Southern California. He is a member of the Burma Buddhist Monastery Association and the Dzogchen Foundation.

A prolific writer whose career spans more than thirty years, Donald has written for children's television and documentaries and has had numerous articles appear in print. An avid motorcyclist, Donald enjoys riding along the Oregon coast. He lives in Portland, Oregon, with his wife and two cats.

NEW WORLD LIBRARY is dedicated to publishing books and other media that inspire and challenge us to improve the quality of our lives and the world.

We are a socially and environmentally aware company, and we strive to embody the ideals presented in our publications. We recognize that we have an ethical responsibility to our customers, our staff members, and our planet.

We serve our customers by creating the finest publications possible on personal growth, creativity, spirituality, wellness, and other areas of emerging importance. We serve New World Library employees with generous benefits, significant profit sharing, and constant encouragement to pursue their most expansive dreams.

As a member of the Green Press Initiative, we print an increasing number of books with soy-based ink on 100 percent postconsumer-waste recycled paper. Also, we power our offices with solar energy and contribute to nonprofit organizations working to make the world a better place for us all.

Our products are available
in bookstores everywhere.
For our catalog, please contact:

New World Library
14 Pamaron Way
Novato, California 94949

Phone: 415-884-2100 or 800-972-6657
Catalog requests: Ext. 50
Orders: Ext. 52
Fax: 415-884-2199
Email: escort@newworldlibrary.com

To subscribe to our electronic newsletter, visit
www.newworldlibrary.com

HELPING TO PRESERVE OUR ENVIRONMENT

7,205
trees were saved

www.newworldlibrary.com

New World Library uses 100% postconsumer-waste recycled paper for our books whenever possible, even if it costs more. During 2009 this choice saved the following precious resources:

ENERGY	WASTEWATER	GREENHOUSE GASES	SOLID WASTE
22 MILLION BTU	3 MILLION GAL.	685,000 LB.	200,000 LB.

Environmental impact estimates were made using the Environmental Defense Fund Paper Calculator @ www.papercalculator.org.